Palladio's Children

Based on many years of personal observation, Habraken's important new book critically examines the role of the architect as a professional descendent of Palladio, and as an heir to his architectural legacy.

Seven innovative and carefully crafted essays explore the widening ideological schism between today's architects, whose core values, identity and education remain rooted in the Renaissance legacy of creating artful "masterpieces," and the practical demands on a profession which acts within an evolving, ubiquitous and autonomous built environment or "field."

Clearly written yet expressing complex evolving ideas, this extended argument opens a new forum of debate across design theory, professional practice and academic issues. Moving the subject on from a historical perspective, Habraken shows how architects are increasingly involved in the design of everyday buildings. This must lead to a reassessment of architects' identities, values and education, and the contribution of the architect in the shaping of the built environment.

N. J. Habraken, Professor Emeritus, Department of Architecture, Massachusetts Institute of Technology (MIT) has enjoyed a worldwide following for four decades. He is the author of a half dozen books, the subject of two recent ones and his recent publication of *The Structure of the Ordinary* (MIT 1998) was widely reviewed internationally. As founding director of the SAR Research Institute and founding chair of the Department of Architecture and Urban Design at Eindhoven Technical University, his research and writing led to the founding of the Open Building Movement.

Jonathan Teicher has edited two previous books by John Habraken. He is a practicing architect and holds an M.Arch. from MIT and two degrees in comparative literature from Washington University. He lectures in architecture and has co-authored a Spon Press title with Stephen Kendall, *Residential Open Building*, which is related to Habraken's work.

Seven essays on everyday environment and the architect

Palladio's Children

N. J. HABRAKEN   EDITED BY JONATHAN TEICHER

Taylor & Francis
Taylor & Francis Group

LONDON • NEW YORK

First published 2005 by Taylor & Francis
2 Park Square, Milton Park, Abingdon, Oxon, OX14 4RN

Simultaneously published in the USA and Canada
by Taylor and Francis
270 Madison Avenue, New York, NY10016

Taylor & Francis is an imprint of the Taylor & Francis Group

Designed and typeset by Sutchinda Rangsi Thompson
Typeset in Didot
Printed and bound in Great Britain by The Cromwell Press, Trowbridge, Wiltshire

British Library Cataloguing in Publication Data
A catalogue record for this book is available from the British Library

Library of Congress Cataloging in Publication Data

Habraken, N. J.
    Palladio's children : essays on everyday environment and the
architect / N.J. Habraken ; edited by Jonathan Teicher.— 1st ed.
        p. cm.
    Includes bibliographical references and index.
    ISBN 0-415-35784-5 (pbk. : alk. paper) — ISBN 0-415-35791-8 (hardback : alk.
paper) 1. Architecture and society. 2. Architecture—Aesthetics. 3. Palladio, Andrea,
1508-1580—Influence. I. Teicher, Jonathan. II. Title.
    NA2543.S6H33 2005

    720'.1'03—dc22
                                                2005009518

ISBN 0-415-35784-5 (hbk)
ISBN 0-415-35791-8 (pbk)

For Julie and Wouter

With thanks to Jonathan for encouragement and patience

Credits

"Towards An Architecture of the Field," first appeared in an earlier version in "Cultivating the Field: About an Attitude When Making Architecture," a Graduation Day Address presented at the Technion – Israel Institute of Technology. © N. John Habraken and the Center for Research, Development and Design in Architecture, Faculty of Architecture and Town Planning, Technion – Israel Institute of Technology, 1993.

The Preface and "About Fields" were previously excerpted in an earlier version in "John Habraken: Palladio's Children," *Folio 06*, Singapore: Department of Architecture, School of Design and Environment, National University of Singapore, 2005.

Illustrations

Except as noted, photographs and drawings are by the author.

1.5 is based on an illustration in Camillo Semenzato's The Rotonda of Andrea Palladio.

1.6 Allan T. Kohl/Art Images for College Teaching. Reprinted with permission.

2.2 + **4.4** KLM Aerocarto NL. Reprinted with permission.

2.4 is based on measured drawings by Paolo Maretto *et al*.

2.5 Oliver Radford, reprinted courtesy of the photographer.

3.1 from the collection of the Harvard-Yenching Library, Harvard University. Reprinted with permission.

3.3 Base map courtesy of the Association Sauvegarde de la Medina, Tunis. Reprinted with permission.

3.5 Drawing by Sir Leonard Woolley et al, courtesy of the University of Pennsylvania Museum. Reprinted with Permission.

3.6 + **3.7** by J. L. Teicher. Reprinted courtesy of the photographer.

Contents

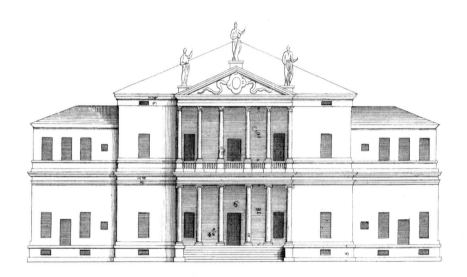

0.1 Country House for Giorgio Cornara
Façade from plate XXXVI of the second book of *The Four Books on Architecture* by Andrea Palladio.

Preface

Across the centuries, despite dramatic changes in artistic and stylistic preferences, we, as architects, still recognize ourselves in the image of Palladio.

Andrea Palladio (1508–1580), born Andrea di Piero, brought forth from the Veneto during the Renaissance a bold new authoritative architecture, free from the medieval constraints of Venice and uncompromising. He published his *œuvre* in his own lifetime, and began a worldwide movement that bears his name. Palladian style no longer guides the profession, but much of what architects do – and how we do it – continues to emulate this undisputed master.

We share another heritage as well, the heritage of master builders acting within living, growing, ubiquitous and autonomous built environment: what we refer to as "the field." Fields comprise built landscapes and the people that inhabit them. For thousands of years, fields have taken root, grown, come into bloom and evolved, sustaining themselves without need of architects or planners.

The architect was traditionally occupied with the monumental palace, villa or church. Yet during the past century, architects became fully immersed in the entirety of the field. This signaled a fundamental and unprecedented shift. The demands of the everyday environment are vastly different from what is required to create the extraordinary. Nevertheless, the profession's self-image, publications and ways of working still cling to its roots in monumental architecture.

In short, there is a disconnect between the way we, as architects, perceive and explain ourselves and what we actually do. As a result, neither our working methods, nor our teachings, nor our values permit the profession to be effective. The resulting conflict confuses everyone: practitioners and clients, teachers and students alike. More importantly, it prevents us from serving and sustaining the field as well as we could. Nor can the ordinary environment nourish us in return. Cut off from the sustenance of the field, we are caught in a self-referential cycle of diminishing returns. With each succeeding generation, architects seem to grow more disoriented, dissatisfied. The backdrop of frenzied or delirious imagery that we create obscures the inevitable recognition of our disjunction.

The seven essays that follow reflect on the state of architecture relative to the everyday environment. They are variations on a theme, ranging from historic interpretation to actual engagement. We are still Palladio's children. We remain his inheritors even as we prepare for the new role thrust upon us by circumstance and necessity, even when we welcome its new opportunities and challenges. The problems of identity and self-justification that we experience in returning to the field are an inevitable result. The better we understand our present condition, the more easily we will adjust to our return to the field. Without denying where we come from, and without rejecting what amid the heritage we carry remains valid.

I considered it worthy of man, who is not born for himself alone but also to be of use to others . . . to expound briefly what . . . seemed to me to be most worthy of consideration, and also the rules that I have followed and still follow when building; so that those who read my books may benefit from what is useful in them and supply for themselves those things (of which perhaps there will be many) which I have overlooked; so that, little by little, one may learn to set aside those strange abuses, barbarous inventions, and pointless expenses and (most importantly) avoid the common failures of various kinds that have been seen in many buildings.

— **ANDREA PALLADIO**, Author's Foreword to *The Four Books on Architecture*

Palladio's children

His villas still speak to us. Their quiet dignity appeals to both lay person and professional. Ancient houses left standing in the countryside display classical façades with columns, entablature, stairs and monumental doors in exquisite proportion that seldom fails to seduce. They evoke nostalgic memories of households living a life of ease and luxury, seemingly so much more noble than our own.

But with Palladio there is more: surprising juxtapositions executed in a relaxed balance of volumes; lucid geometry; impeccable proportions; and the sure craftsmanship of simple details in masonry, in modest brick and plaster with occasional stone. And always, there is the innate good taste of buildings at ease with themselves. Such qualities silence any hastily formed associations and analogies. They transcend our notions of function, history and iconography. As architects, we recognize a colleague, a guild master who, in spite of more than four hundred and fifty years' distance, we yearn to see as one of us.

We know, deep down, when form is good. Ordinary built environment has its own ways. It is guided by gravity, by territorial control and no less by customs of construction. Architecture such as Palladio's, set against the canvas of such ordinary fabric, makes everyday environment shine. In so doing, it is rendered timeless, free of contemporary style and symbolism. We recognize that quality in his work.

1.1–1.4 Palladio's imprint
1.1 Villa Rotonda, view from the entrance gate.

1.2 Villa Rotonda, stair at the back of the building, close to the retaining wall.

1.3 Villa Rotonda, detail of porch steps showing column bases.

1.4 Villa Rotonda, sculpture viewed from the porch.

Others, equally impressive in their own ways, built in that remarkable Renaissance era. There are Donato Bramante's innovations, Filippo Brunelleschi's daring and poetic craftsmanship, Leon Battista Alberti's intellectual illumination. In Venice, there is also Mauro Codussi's sure yet unobtrusive assertion of power; and, in another culture, Sinan's orchestration of monumental projects. These architects also produced lasting monuments that reveal unquestionable mastery. And yet, there is a clear distinction: we see them as individuals attached to their time.

It is not just the work that attracts us. Palladio, as a colleague, has outlasted even Modernism's attempt to sweep the field clean. We no longer follow his classical precepts, but he is with us still. We recognize in Palladio's work a familiar attitude toward making architecture, one that we share. We still view ourselves much in the way he may have seen himself.

In examining how we explain ourselves as architects today, we do well to look first at Palladio. He was the first to publish his *œuvre* during his own lifetime. It was an unprecedented act with far-ranging results.[1]

A few decades earlier, Sebastiano Serlio (1475–1554) had published a selection of buildings that would establish the canons of Renaissance architecture.[2] Unlike Leon Battista Alberti's intellectual reflections on the nature of architecture in a new era, Serlio's designs were intended to enlighten and inspire peers and clients alike. Serlio was not the first after Vitruvius Pollio, the Roman architect who wrote around the time of Jesus, to show examples of architecture, but the quality of Serlio's drawings and the variety of subjects set a new standard. Above all, Serlio's are books of drawings: The text is secondary.

Palladio had previously (1554) published a popular scholarly guide to Roman architecture, *Le Antichità di Roma.*[3] In *The Four Books on Architecture,* Palladio, like those before him, professes to follow the traditional format set by Vitruvius in *The Ten Books on*

Architecture. Yet while Palladio adopts the picture book format of Serlio, he comes across as a practicing architect and a former master mason erecting buildings to exacting standards. He informs and educates by reporting on ancient buildings he himself has measured and by showing his own designs – most of which have actually been built.

Only the second book gives us his renowned villas and urban palaces. But the publication as a whole projects a consistency in style and a preoccupation with balanced composition. As a result, *The Four Books on Architecture* was primarily understood as a representation of Palladio's way of working. In Serlio's writings, the author is rather academic, full of ideas but lacking practical judgment. But Palladio's books show a master builder at work. He is occupied with matters of style and proportion and construction. He is working for real clients.

The innovative nature of Palladio's publication was not lost on his readers. *The Four Books on Architecture* came to be seen as the record of a personal *œuvre* and, as such, of a new way of defining architecture.

In the course of time, after many others, Le Corbusier would also follow Palladio's example, recording his own twentieth-century work. In fact, Le Corbusier did so with a vengeance. He published the buildings, but also notebook sketches and notes, observations and ideas. New volumes of his ongoing record appeared every few years.[4] They greatly reinforced a popular view of architecture as the story of gifted and successful individuals. More than ever, having one's work published – preferably during one's lifetime, and including cocktail napkin sketches – became the defining mark of arrival: of admission to the inner circle of those who define architecture.

Today, it is hard to exaggerate the importance of the published *œuvre* in establishing what architecture means to us; the ways in which publication shapes perception, and also how we view the architect.

Such was the absolute authority of Palladio's published work that for centuries the mere act of publication lent credibility to subsequent generations of architects. As a multitude of monographs and web sites unleashes an endless torrent of project information, the prestige associated with publication is now on the wane. Such sources less and less represent accolades of excellence, and more and more present uncritical vehicles of marketing and self-promotion.

Yet prestige and personal vanity are the least significant aspects of published architecture. Far more significant is the fact that visual representation of the building, rather than its actual presence in the field, has come to define what architecture is – and what it is not. The number of signature buildings and places we know intimately through published or projected images far exceeds the number we have experienced in real space. We know the buildings, but not their context. Visitors experience an environment in which the building resides. Readers do not. The common references of the architectural profession reside in a common domain that is no longer a space – a city, or a country – but within the media of representation, themselves.

Here again, Palladio was a pioneer. We may assume he had his *œuvre* printed to inform his peers in Rome and Florence of his contribution to the new way of making architecture. The stylistic world they were creating was neither Venetian, nor Roman, nor Florentine. Soon, it would not be solely Italian. As Palladio's example came to inform his peers far beyond the Alps, the printed image bound together a new profession that shared an architecture without a context.

Classicism and neo-classicism bound the profession to a broader social class defined by privilege, taste and education, a class that also included lawyers, prelates, savants, statesmen and noblemen. Architects were no longer defined as Venetian or Parisian, Italian or Anglo-Saxon. Eventually, with the rise of the International Movement, the professional community acquired an identity apart; it has subsequently become increasingly self-referential. Architecture went from identifying a locality or a culture to "*-isms*" that identified groups of practitioners who shared a way of making. It has finally ended up as the story of a grab bag of talented individuals, assembled however the individual historian or critic sees fit. Architects are no longer selected on the basis of their native place or people, but for their reputation within the worldwide network of *cognoscenti*.

If, finally, architecture is what architects do, here again it was the master architect Palladio – no doubt unwittingly – who came first, on the strength of his book: Prior to *Palladian architecture,* no architecture had been named after a single practitioner.

●●●

Palladio's woodblock prints indicate no context. We remain unaware of abutting public spaces or neighbors. We see neither landscape nor topography in the representation of the villas.

In the case of the Villa Almerico-Capra, best known as the Villa Rotonda, Palladio informs us that the site offers beautiful views in all directions, that the building is placed on a small hill with easy access. But he informs us neither of the masterly way he orches-trated the approach to the building nor how he provided it with access to the surrounding estate. In fact, he shows only a building plan, a section and a façade.

This is typical of the entire representation of his *œuvre*: Palladio tells us about his clients. He recounts how noble and important they are: emphasizing that he reports on real buildings built for real people. But the buildings themselves are represented as abstract models divorced from site or context.

Palladio does not deny that a building should be well placed in relation to a road, a hill, a river or the orbit of the sun. In the tradition of Vitruvius, he devotes several pages to the issue of choosing a good and healthy site. But the architecture that Palladio was conveying to his peers in Rome and Florence had to do principally with the geometry and composition of buildings. The actual topic of *The Four Books on Architecture* is how to compose good buildings.

The non-site-specific graphic presentation of architectural objects made Palladio's work eminently useful for distant designers and clients. It was left to them to decide how to adjust these models to accommodate environments and cultures of which Palladio could scarcely have dreamed.

We still live with the ambiguity of this legacy. Architects up to the present day habitually provide minimal information about site or context: as little as they can get away with when the setting is ordinary. Architectural photographers, editors and authors routinely keep us in the dark about surrounding everyday environment. In urban and suburban settings, Palladio's example is followed to the letter, and for the same reason: the ongoing conversation in which published buildings participate is not local. It is a dialogue carried out within a distantly scattered network of peers. Architecture, from Palladianism onwards, has largely been a matter of exquisite signature objects. Site and context are brought to bear to the extent that they serve to heighten the audience's appreciation of the dexterity of the author.

Paradoxically, contemporary architects simultaneously participate in another decidedly non-Palladian tradition, in which the building grows from the landscape, as opposed to being set as an object in it. This *wrightian* site-driven way of consciously shaping

and placing form – subsequently adopted by Alvar Aalto, Sigurd
Lewerentz and Alvaro Siza, among many others – connects to the
age-old tradition of hands-on master building and vernacular
building in immediate connection to the land and its local material
resources. This is also part of our architectural sensibility. It further
increases the tension between the local act and the global dialogue
in which our publications engage. Photographs of Frank Lloyd
Wright's Falling Water cannot adequately convey how the building
relates to the land. And the more such architecture specifically
responds to the rise and fall of the land, to rock outcroppings or
specimen trees, the less the design becomes exportable. This is one
reason why emulation of Wright is so often disappointing: A
building conceived in dialogue with the land does not travel as
easily as a building whose parts relate only to one another. The first
must be conveyed as a way of working, the latter can be transported
as an object.

The well-sited object that is expertly placed in context – rather
than grown from it – comes from a venerable and widespread tradition. The most conspicuous example is monumental architecture,
which throughout history has tended to establish symmetrical self-
containment. In a humbler vein, much of the North American rural
and suburban tradition is one of wooden boxes erected along
streets or in the landscape. In earlier times, they were impermanent,
lifted from their foundations and rolled on logs to new locations as
need arose.

The Palladian approach places itself within this tradition. If
Palladio's wood print images suggest models, his architectural purpose was likewise to objectify the building, to distinguish it from
the landscape.

Perhaps none of Palladio's buildings is as self-contained as the
Villa Rotonda. It is sited with great sophistication. From the gate at
the public road, the visitor is led through a narrow driveway cut

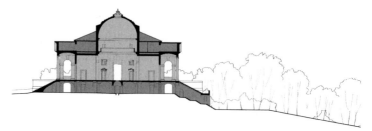

1.5 Villa Rotonda, section showing the basement floor with access to farmland below the retaining wall. Based on an illustration in Camillo Semenzato's *The Rotonda of Andrea Palladio.*

through a rim of the hill, sloping upwards. Ascending on axis between the walls, one first sees the building's monumental façade straight on. It is elevated, tightly framed by the walls of the entryway. [Fig. 1.1.] As one attains the level of the building, space opens to the left and right. Although the monumental steps of the portico lie directly ahead along the axis followed, one cannot continue straight ahead: the driveway splits and turns to access them sideways. This dramatic approach establishes a firm major axis for the perfect multiple symmetry of the building and the uniformity of its four elevations.[5]

The portico stairs of two other façades descend close to a retaining wall, where the land abruptly drops some five meters. No attempt is made to mediate between the ample descent offered by the stairs and the contradictory abrupt halt called by the wall a few feet from it. [Fig. 1.2] From within, the basement floor exits downward under the porticos, through the retaining walls, discharging directly on grade below. These two hidden exits are as ingenious as they are utilitarian: Unseen from the main floor, they assure servants and laborers access to the surrounding land, while also allowing four identical porticos to remain indifferent to varying site conditions.[6]

Formally, the building remains self-contained. The Villa Rotonda assumes a vantage point the way a visitor might to survey the view on all sides. It dominates the land while not becoming rooted in it. Palladio's handling of site is every bit as skillful and innovative as Wright's.[7] But Palladio achieves the opposite effect: The building ingeniously uses the unique site conditions to make all the necessary functional connections; nevertheless, it is set like a stone upon the hill. From Le Corbusier came the ultimate expression of this attitude: the building on *pilotis* hovering over an immaculate lawn.[8]

Given the strong tradition that binds contemporary architectural representation, it is hardly surprising that publications about Palladio's work – and particularly his villas – exclude information on siting and context. Yet the modern representation of the freestanding building, with its sensibility of implicit detachment, is decidedly different from what Palladio sought to convey. Again, the Villa Rotonda is instructive: In books, postcards and architects' slides, it is most frequently depicted in diagonal perspective, so that we can see two elevations at the same time. To obtain that diagonal perspective view, an endless stream of photographers now wanders across the lawn to a far corner of the site, where no path extends. Following the suburban real estate sales tradition, this view maximizes the building's "curb appeal." But it ignores the axial monumentality Palladio wanted the visitor to experience.

While we follow in Palladio's footsteps, we reject the axiality of his architecture.

Or perhaps it is better to say that we feel so close to Palladio that we are simply unaware of the ways in which we have grown profoundly different.

●●●

1.6 Villa Rotonda, diagonal perspective. Today, we prefer to show buildings in diagonal perspective views to heighten the "curb appeal" of the architectural image. Photograph © Allan T. Kohl/Art Images for College Teaching. Reprinted with permission.

We may assume that Palladio's desire to write stemmed in part from his desire to contribute to the ongoing dialogue among his peers in Rome and Florence because, for all of its Byzantine splendor, Venice was a backwater far removed from the vortex of the Renaissance. Venice harbored no little resistance to the new "Roman architecture."[9] In publishing, Palladio engaged in a "network culture" within a social body whose members were not bound to any single location, but were dispersed across a variety of local cultures.

The architecture of the Roman Empire from which Palladio drew inspiration was similarly part of a network culture. Roman building types – temples, villas, baths, palaces and fortresses, aqueducts and colonnaded streets – were found throughout the Mediterranean world and beyond. They extended along trade and military routes maintained by the Imperium; indifferent to local architectures, but akin to one another.

Following the model of Hellenic colonial architecture, Roman architecture was often introduced by colonists and expatriates or else imposed by imperial administrations. Or it might be emulated by local elites who aspired to Roman citizenship and identified with a more universal and more powerful culture. In symbolic terms, the Roman presence was surely dominant, and in Western history it has come to exclusively represent the architecture of its time. Yet as the archaeological record shows, the Roman presence was spatially dispersed, its buildings surrounded by local vernacular, including vernacular public buildings.

As the Imperium disintegrated, the network culture sustained by Roman roads was eventually eroded by successive waves of invading barbarians from the north and later by the new Islamic culture from the east. Its far-flung architecture fell into ruin or was overgrown by vernacular fabrics, to be "rediscovered" by Italian Renaissance architects after a millennium of neglect. From their innovative interpretations of that ancient architecture, a new network-based architecture emerged. This architectural component of the comprehensive culture of classicism was, of course, heavily influenced by Palladio's work.

Classically-inspired architecture would eventually be found throughout Western Europe. As in Roman times, classical buildings were again erected as isolated presences surrounded by a vast variety of local vernacular buildings. Classicism spread across eastern Europe, through St. Petersburg and onto the plains between Prussia and Moscow, dotting the landscape with uncounted country estates. The estate of Chekov's *Uncle Vanya* – which we can only imagine built in the classical manner – would have co-existed with the onion domes of the local village church.

And classicism spread throughout the North American continent and to other far-flung colonies as well. In the typical clapboard architecture of New England villages we find wooden courthouses, town halls, and churches with Palladian façades crafted with great skill and excellent proportions. Palladian colonnaded porches adorned antebellum mansions throughout the Confederate States of America. And of course, it is hard to find a Federal era state house in the United States that was not built in the classical manner.[10]

Again, the role of printed architecture in this development must not be underestimated. Copies of books by Palladio and Sebastiano Serlio remained relatively rare, but the many derivative pattern books covered every detail and variation possible. As a result, local builders who had never been to Europe, let alone in the Veneto, could follow the way of Palladio. By studying the publications, it was possible without travel to become expert in a foreign way of designing. One could learn to build in that manner – at least, with respect to symmetry and proportion and disposition of parts in the principal façade – without being taught by someone who had seen extant examples in Greece, Italy, France or England.

In contrast to the Greek and Roman cultures of colonialism, the network culture of neo-classicism did not represent a single territorial power. Nor was it named after a people. Encompassing the vast British Empire but reaching far beyond it, neo-classicism represented an elite transcending political boundaries, united by education in the arts, history, Latin and Greek. Although neo-classicism did not exclude people of modest birth, it rested on the intellectual tradition of those who held power. What they shared was found on both sides of national boundaries and across battle lines.

The architecture embraced by this elite could be the product of commoners such as Inigo Jones, gentleman architects like Christopher Wren, or gifted amateurs like Thomas Jefferson. But its fundamental reliance on the example of printed images of buildings and their details and orders continued a way of learning and connecting already initiated by Palladio and his peers.

Many decades later, International Style[11] architects would again seek out one another across national boundaries, transcend local customs to compare notes and find common ground. Like their predecessors, they too implanted their buildings in the midst of the local vernacular.[12]

But there was a critical difference: For all that Renaissance architects valued innovation, they never failed to invoke the authority of ancient architecture to justify their own, often very different, work. The ancients became the acknowledged wellspring of all good architecture. Classicistic architecture stayed within this tradition and traced its roots back to that same authority.

Modernist architecture could not refer to such heritage, nor did it want to. In rejecting all extraneous constraints, it elevated Renaissance love for innovation and *novitas* to an end in itself. And so, architecture became the jealously guarded property of the professional class that invented it. Lacking any external higher authority, it relied on promotion of the avant garde. In effect, the profession took on the world at large. No longer part of a more encompassing society, and wanting to escape the constraints and values of a powerful bourgeoisie, an international professional network now became an alternative field for peers to operate in: it became a goal unto itself.

●●●

Succeeding generations added elaborately crafted engravings to later editions of Palladio's *Four Books on Architecture*. But the modern eye is not particularly excited by the lavish details and clever shadings made possible by use of tools like the hand-held burin or technical advances in printing. The sparse and abstract rendering in Palladio's own simple woodblock prints sympathizes with the equally restrained illustrations in Le Corbusier's and Ozenfant's first publications on a shoestring budget.[13] In all cases, pure geometry speaks, unencumbered by indications of material, color or texture.

We recognize the same abstraction in Palladio's villas. Sculpture occasionally placed on roof parapets and at entry stairs only serves to highlight the simple stucco walls and moldings pared down to their essence. Architects do not as readily identify with Palladio's more elaborately detailed and decorated urban palaces in Vicenza or with his ornate Venetian churches. No less admirable for the skills with which they were brought about, the latter speak to a sensibility more removed from ours . . . We prefer to remember our cathedrals stark and white.

In equating Palladio's unadorned exteriors with Modernism's early days, we discount the frescoes found in Palladian interiors. In Palladio's day, a balance was struck between ornament and plain sculptural abstraction. Structure was never expressed for its own sake; nor was authentic portrayal of materials a consideration. Palladio frequently worked with budget constraints, and he unapologetically executed columns in thrifty plastered brick or stacked from sculpted segments when resources did not allow them to be turned from a single block of marble. Brick columns might conceal their structure and express stone; structural stone might be painted. Such dematerialization of built structure is part of the western architectural tradition, and we subsequently see, on the American continent as well as the Russian plains, fluted columns skillfully crafted in wood and, finally, with the machine age in New York City, cast in iron or molded in terra cotta.

Nevertheless, the beauty of materials, their grain and color, did not escape our forebears: Venice itself displays decorative stone in many colors. Byzantine architecture extended the Roman tradition of setting polished slabs of marbles of different colors to show their veins in symmetrical juxtaposition, not to express structure, but to conceal it and create a skin. Subsequently, as Modernism came to the fore, ornament was eliminated and the balance to be struck was re-formulated: it was between structural expression and display of materials on one hand, and sculptural de-materialization on the other.

For subsequent generations of post-World War II architects, a new notion was introduced: revisionist sentiment saw in the vestiges of Greek temples buildings of blindingly crystalline marble. It admired Gothic cathedrals in ochre and buff sandstone stained by wind and water. Henceforth, bearing structure was to be similarly expressed throughout the building, its tactile and visual qualities preempting ornament both in the façade and in the interior. This sentiment was cloaked in an odd guise of rationality and moral integrity. We still nurture that sentiment today although, rationally, we know full well that the Romans liked to sheath their utilitarian concrete and rubble engineering in marble panels of many colors, that the Parthenon was painted from top to bottom, as were major portions of the cathedrals in the Île de France.

Today we have grown somewhat jaded, accustomed to large and perfect surfaces of steel, glass or marble clothing a building's skeleton. It is hard to imagine the awe and wonder of ancient Egyptians who gazed upon the perfectly flat triangles of colossal dimensions formed by the newly finished pyramids. By contrast, in their eroded state, it is the marvel of layer upon layer of room-sized blocks lifted by unknown means, stacked with great precision and expressing gravity as no other human structure could, that fascinates us. Although seldom expressed in monumental architecture in the past, the desire to let structural material speak directly, to have it reveal the channeling of gravity in the joining of heavy stones and timber, explains the particular attraction of ruins for the modern eye.

In that light, the stone walls of the Incas seem sophisticated and exceptional for the incomprehensible matching of random shapes without mediating mortar: they were intended to be seen that way. In contrast, a finished cathedral sculpted with devotion in ever-varying detail clothes its structure rather than emphasizing it. But where time has taken its toll and the joints between stones show, we see the beauty of structural form regaining its identity. And perhaps admire the more the sculptor's skill.

Thus the desire to see actual material work with gravity while showing its grains and natural colors without decoration or sheathing seems new. Its pursuit by such masters as Frank Lloyd Wright, Sigurd Lewerentz, Alvar Aalto and Antoni Gaudí – even the maverick classicist Edwin Lutyens – speaks to our sensibility as much as early Modernism's white boxes. But while the latter come from our Palladian tradition, the unadorned expression of structure finds little precedence in architectural history as it was taught us.

Its roots are hardly obscure, but they lie in vernacular building.

We remain caught between the vernacular and the formal. In this tension between the ways of Palladio and those of the field, we find evidence of the dual heritage we carry and with which we must still come to terms.

●●●

Vicenza, where Palladio lived and worked most of his life, was part of the Venetian *"terra firma."* By the end of the fifteenth century, Venice's extensive mainland territories, acquired in fifteenth century political and military engagements, stretched all the way to the Adda River.[14] In contrast to Rome, Milan and Florence, Venice was a republic. For a thousand years, successive generations of a handful of families had filled posts in government, in the navy, in embassies and trading houses throughout the Mediterranean. The governance of Venice was carefully balanced to avoid supremacy by

1.7 Venice, façades of Gothic "palaces" along the Canal Grande.

any single clan. To the extent that the oligarchy included nobility, their fortunes were largely founded on trade as opposed to territorial feudal power. Now, at a time when Venice's naval supremacy and trading network was beginning to shrink, investment capital began to flow inland and land-based enterprises gained importance. Most of the land around Padua in the sixteenth century, for instance, was owned by Venetians.[15]

Vicenza, in contrast, was not colonized by Venetian capital. Palladio's private clients came primarily from the oligarchy of Vicenza itself. Controlling the wealthiest province on the mainland, they traditionally ran their own commercial and agricultural enterprises, thereby maintaining independence from Venetian money. This provided a new clientele for an innovative architect. As Howard Burns explains: "It gave Palladio a multitude of effective patrons, not just one effective princely patron . . . [which was] the normal situation in Rome or Florence."[16]

These patrons needed something different from the *palazzi* along the canals of Venice. Those houses were products of a Gothic vernacular tradition, inseparable from the urban fabric. They did not lend themselves to exportation to the mainland. For centuries, master carpenters and masons had devoted themselves to producing, extending and maintaining this fabric. They did not know how to produce something divorced from it.

Palladio's genius seized upon this problem as an opportunity. Through inventive modification, he coined a new kind of building, freed from many constraints and customs of an age-old urban tradition. The Palladian villa was tailored to the needs of a new style of living and working. Abandoning extant urban fabric and moving into the countryside proved essential for this innovation. The building no longer formed the backdrop to social spaces like *canale* or *campo*, nor was it tied in to a network of streets and alleyways. [Figs. 2.3 and 2.4.] The villa was seen only by those invited to visit and willing to take the journey. Out of town, in the open country, client and architect were compelled to jointly fashion something radically new.

In this new situation, a more intimate, less hierarchical relationship between client and architect came about. As a young, promising and charming mason, Andrea di Piero was sponsored by Count Gian Giorgio Trissino. It was Trissino who eventually renamed him "Palladio" after Pallas Athena.[17] Palladio gradually rose in station, eventually joining his patron as a member of the Accademia in Vicenza. Palladio was thus put in direct touch with potential clients with whom he could share the quest for knowledge and learning typical of the nascent culture arising in that entrepreneurial city.[18]

In this aspect, too, Palladio's position was more "modern" than that of his peers elsewhere. Most members of the new professional class of architects that emerged during the Renaissance still worked for the traditional patrons: the church and the nobility. In Rome, no cardinal, pope or prince dreamed of inviting his architect – no matter how intimate their personal relationship – into his social circle.

Removed from the social and contextual constraints of urban fabric, the private dwelling provided a freedom to redefine and to demonstrate not offered by any other kind of commission. Realizing the vision depended solely on mutual trust and respect between client and architect in a less hierarchical relationship.

Withdrawal from urban civic presence has become a residential norm in our times. Contemporary masterpiece dwellings are private to an extent unthinkable to the Renaissance mind. Removed from urban fabric, they may not even shelter an extended household of family and servants. Nor do they occupy sites prominently visible in the landscape. Rather, they are single family dwellings, often hidden in woods at the end of unmarked driveways or behind unmarked walls; for all practical purposes they are invisible to those not expressly invited.

Such villas participate in the broader social realm only to the extent that their occupants entertain relatives, friends and visitors; they exist as works of architecture only to the extent they are published. As such, they figure in a network culture, but not in a specific place. Some iconic residences may today be visited as museums; nonetheless, their entry into the public sphere is entirely due to renown acquired through publication.

This collection of the unseen shapes to a significant extent our understanding of contemporary architecture; and it exists by grace of the printed page.[19] Only publication can reconcile the client's desire for privacy with the architect's desire to be known by his or her work. Accordingly, renowned architects are now introduced to clients via published work. For architect and client alike, the printed image has replaced the shared urban space of earlier days.

To what extent did Palladio seek through his publications to make visible to potential clients and other citizens of Venice an *œuvre* so radically removed from their common civic space? Perhaps he never had this in mind, at all. Perhaps Palladio published for the reason architects do today: to gain recognition: not among the local community with whom we work and live, but among a network of distant peers.

●━●━●

Inventione became a key term in the architectural discourse of the Renaissance.[20] The conditions that led Palladio to define a new architecture on the *terra firma* of the Venetian Republic were ideal for what his profession and his clients were trying to achieve: something truly new to sweep away local tradition.

Human creativity is irrepressible and mindless repetition is unnatural. Since no human act can precisely replicate precedent, all design involves some invention. Conversely, invention lies not in denial of all norms, but rather in interpreting in a novel way what is already collectively accepted.

Yet those who sought to resurrect classical ways were obsessed by the desire to invent. Within a society steeped in medieval tradition, embracing the ways of working of antiquity provided a context for innovation. Classical precedent was not to be copied. It was rather expected to provide the systemic order and standard against which invention could be measured. Lesser talents might have feared the stifling effect of surveying ancient structures with exacting patience, month after month. But as Palladio and other Renaissance masters understood, new constraints within a newly adopted system of classical parts assured fresh invention.

The urge to be original at all costs is now a guiding force and compulsion of architecture. The contemporary private house in the woods seen only by the photographer's lens is the ideal setting in which to indulge it. But the attitude has now become an almost universal precondition for recognition. In recognizing a similar compulsion to innovate, but seeing only similarities, we seriously misread Palladio.

There is a fundamental difference between our own *originality* and the *inventione* of the master architect of the Veneto. Contemporary architects view building without recourse to urban typology or building culture as an opportunity for a *tabula rasa*: That clean slate is now believed to provide the ideal conditions for creativity. But Palladio accepted two systemic constraints that allowed him to be truly inventive: the first was the classical orders.

The second constraint was local vernacular tradition, both in terms of form and in employment of local craft strongly tied to it. Stucco on brick was a common building finish. The red tiled roof was found on farm and city houses alike. Tripartite division of the façade – the open middle bay flanked by windows on both sides – characterized the Gothic palace and was part of the vernacular *laguna* building tradition of Venice. Small rectangular windows in the entablature of the façade are of a similarly vernacular origin, a common device to introduce natural light into the attic. The columniated portico was a feature of antiquity. In nearby Padua, Palladio's birthplace, the streets were lined with porticos in his time, as they are today.

What we admire in Palladio is therefore not a rejection of precedent, but the sure and relaxed way in which he fused the already known, the newly found and the rediscovered into something of great dignity.

A taste for invention, understood in this fertile way, was very much part of the Renaissance movement. No one before Donato Bramante had combined the dome with the classical colonnade in precisely the way he did. It established his Tempietto in Rome as a model for successive generations. In Florence, we admire Filippo Brunelleschi for his astonishing dome, rooted in the Gothic tradition; but no less for his celebrated portico at the Foundling Hospital (Ospedale Degli Innocenti). There, slender column, wall, arch and vault are executed with sensitivity, acquiring an astonishing poetry in their juxtapositions, guided by a transparent geometry. And of course, the work of Leon Battista Alberti, who first and most forcefully interpreted and reintroduced ancient tradition, is full of invention in its own right.

●●●

The emulation of Palladio's way of working produced "Palladian" architecture, ushering in the now-common use of an individual architect as eponymous hero for an architecture.

The individuals who conceived buildings and towns prior to the fifteenth century were not anonymous, their names were frequently recorded for posterity. We know, for instance, that it was Ictinus, in association with Callicrates, who built the Parthenon. Yet it seems reasonable to view this temple – so fundamentally part of an established typology, unique features and sublime proportions notwithstanding – as the product of a culture rather than of an individual. Indeed, our penchant for crediting an individual architect with the design of a remarkable building arose during the Renaissance.

Surely, gifted individuals now forgotten participated in the creation of familiar ancient monuments and towns. But where buildings and towns were strongly tied to typology, who deserves the credit? After fire destroyed Chartres Cathedral in 1194, more than a dozen different master builders consecutively arrived to rebuild it with their teams. The process took thirty-six years. The sequence of their participation has been recreated through painstaking archaeological scholarship.[21] Yet the primary involve-ment of so great a number of actors frustrates any attempt to credit design to an individual.

In Roman times, was the seminal designer of the colony the conquering general or the political patron or the nobleman who steered the sacred plow along the periphery of a new settlement to establish its boundaries and the location of its gates? Or perhaps the surveyor who laid out the street pattern, set out the colony's extents, as well as the correct relation of *cardo* and *decumanus* to the sun's path. Or should we perhaps credit the person who performed the necessary ritual to do justice to the gods, who lit the sacred fire and directed the offerings prior to the plowing of the periphery? Or perhaps the augur who found the exact spot chosen by the gods and signified by the flight of birds?[22]

Ancient architecture is named after peoples: we speak of Greek, Roman and Egyptian architecture. Subsequently, we largely mark religious classifications, speaking of *romanesque*, *gothic* and *islamic* architecture. This introduces a naming of styles not necessarily connected to a specific people or geographic location. Beginning with the Renaissance, stylistic names – *baroque, neo-classical, neo-gothic, modernist* – begin to reflect preferences among individual architects and their clients rather than entire cultures.

Even so, in historiography, identification of the architectural object only gradually shifts towards the name of the individual designer. The idea that architecture actually flows from architects – rather than from a people, its culture, and its setting within a nation, a region and a landscape – achieved currency only with the Renaissance. Henceforth, in classifying buildings, the histori-ographer begins to attach the names of architects to them. Well after Palladian architecture, there is *miesian* (named after Ludwig Mies van der Rohe), *wrightian*, or *corbusian* architecture.

Architects now aspire to become eponymous heroes and household names. But that ambition, by its very universality, has proven illusory. Any grouping defies the culture of individual expression: how many architects would aspire to inclusion in a style defined by another?

Consequently, architectural classification is now strictly designer by designer – at least among historians, architects and the *cognoscenti*. Yet it is still better to ask a New Yorker "How do you get to the Guggenheim?" than to inquire how to find Frank Lloyd Wright's museum. And who in Manhattan identifies the Chrysler or Woolworth buildings by the names William Van Alen or Cass Gilbert? In day-to-day life, buildings, modest and monumental alike, continue to find their place as landmarks in a society's fabric, marking a city or a neighborhood, or a simple function while, conversely, location and context confirm their identity.

Yet the monograph most readily reflects the way architects and architectural historians, theorists and critics would have society see the world. From this perspective, a building's whereabouts may be circumstantial. Nor do attempts to describe, group or compare buildings by function in "building type" studies seem to advance our understanding of architecture.

In terms of the self-image of the architectural profession, labeling an architecture "Palladian" was an act of supreme significance. It distinguished the designer from the indissoluble unity of environmental form and culture that had until then brought forth buildings and entire urban fields, embodying skills and knowledge. From Palladio on, architecture has been identified with individual architects. Everything else – the entirety of the ordinary built field where form, inhabitant and maker are functionally integrated and semantically joined – has remained obscure or self-evident. This has inevitably led to the emancipation – and the isolation – of an entire professional culture from the integrated field of form and people.

We are the product of that separation. Our traditions of designing and discussing architecture and writing its history – the fundamental way we see ourselves and our work – have grown from it.

It is hard to accept that an alternative view reigned for millennia, or may again replace it in future.

Leaving the field

Renaissance architects took the ordinary built environment all around them for granted. Today, by contrast, architects concern themselves with the existence and quality of everyday environment. Ordinary environment is now viewed as a problem to which the architect must contribute a solution. This shift in perspective has had tremendous consequences for the environment in which we live and the profession we have become. To facilitate the discussion of built environment in this context, I use the term *field* to denote the context as well as purpose of the architectural enterprise: the urban, suburban and rural environments in which and for which we act when we design and build. Fields are autonomous entities. Their complex dynamics extend beyond any single discipline or area of study.

Built environment comes close to the concept of fields. However, apart from being an unwieldy term, it tends to refer to a physical entity only. In its totality, it comprises buildings, the spaces formed by them, roads, railways and other infrastructures serving them and squares, parks and gardens relating to them. But it still leaves out people. Built environment cannot sustain itself without a population. Once abandoned, nature reclaims it; eventually, it is reduced to ruins.

The term *field* encompasses all. Fields are only conceivable as coherent and enduring physical entities because they are inhabited, subject to and continuously reshaped by the unending actions and

2.1–2.4 The endurance of fields

2.1 Amsterdam, part of the partially completed "Jordaan" neighborhood, from a map by Balthasar Florisz. van Berckenrode, ca. 1625. Created in the Third Extension of Amsterdam, the Jordaan neighborhood stands apart from the houses of the well-to-do, which line the three major canals. The Jordaan neighborhood was intended for tradesmen and artisans. Its streets and canals followed the existing subdivision of the countryside by ditches.

2.2 Amsterdam, the same portion of the "Jordaan" neighborhood in an aerial photograph about 350 years later. Photograph © KLM Aerocarto NL. Reprinted with permission.

2.3 Venice, San Polo District, detail from a map by Jacopo Barbari ca. 1539.

2.4 Venice, detail after a contemporary survey by Paolo Maretto. This plan features the four buildings along the Canal Grande indicated in Fig 2.4. The building plans are typical, featuring a large central hall open to front and back with rooms on both sides and a stairway to the ground floor giving access to canal and back streets.

interventions of the people who live within the material fabric. It is also difficult to conceive of people – real vital physical entities as well – without their habitat and the urban, suburban and rural places shaped by them. In speaking of fields and comparing their properties, we recognize this inseparable co-existence.

We are so accustomed to living with the field that the very wholeness of our existence within that material envelope is too common to be noted explicitly. Yet we do not simply interact with other human beings: we do so while positioning ourselves within structures and spaces that reflect and mold social relationships. And those spaces in turn are modified to suit our presence: We shift furniture, work doors, elevators, faucets and light switches, furnish and decorate, buy, sell or rent property. We decide on interventions of our own or debate larger ones to be taken collectively.

The sheer size and complexity of a constantly pulsating field like Manhattan with its manifestation of life and energy are astounding. Visiting ancient teeming fields where the automobile never dominated, we recognize a similar complexity and energy. Fabrics like those of Cairo have existed for over a thousand years. The precincts of the tourist bazaar, the Al Hazar and Ibn Touloun mosques and the Bab Zuweila Gate reveal, in their spatial organization, common ancestry with the field of Ur, alive four thousand years ago. And new fields are created all the time. Contemporary suburbs spring from a similar unity of human life and physical shelter.

The constant interaction between living and inert matter lends fields an organic quality and makes it impossible to separate inhabitation from intervention. In the connection between life and its physical shelter, there exists a continuum from an individual pulling a chair closer to the table to a town council deciding to expand the urban fabric. Fields are too encompassing, too durable and too complex to be simply considered artifacts produced by us.

A wide spectrum of fields is manifest. It encompasses the notorious squatter settlements in the developing world that produce, over time, the vast unplanned neighborhoods ringing the world's most populated cities – Istanbul, Cairo, Mexico City, Shanghai and Jakarta, to name just a few. There, small contractors and local manufacturers sustain a constant pace of improvement and expansion. At the other end of the spectrum, there proliferate the developer-built suburbs, housing projects developed for sale or rent and high-rise buildings so characteristic of the modern city.

Designers are beholden to the field: it shapes our intervention far more than our work can transform it. Yet for several generations, architects fervently believed that fields could be not only designed, but invented, and that the quality and the very perpetuation of fields depended on the design professions. Any assessment of the way we see ourselves as architects and define our mission must take into consideration the unity of the field.

●●●

The Venetian field had been blooming for centuries when Palladio, aided by circumstance and joined by his patrons, escaped its powerful constraints by building inland villas. In terms of building typology, there is scant connection between Palladio's villas and the buildings that line the Venetian canals. Even his Vicenza *palazzi*, embedded in local fabric, are not as free and new as the Villa Rotonda.

Later in life, Palladio did in fact build two churches in Venice. They were built on the outskirts of Venice proper. San Giorgio Maggiore stands on the island of San Giorgio opposite the Piazza San Marco. The wide stretch of water is open all the way to the renowned Doge's Palace, and the building's façade marks it in a convincing and elegant way. Behind the church's doors another world is hidden: one of cool geometric clarity, impervious to the tumult of urban walls and roofs and restless waters.

The Church of the Redentore, Palladio's second Venetian church, is on the nearby island of Giudecca. It too relates to the island opposite by its façade. It stands on the waterfront, self-contained, an object of extraordinary presence in the midst of humble and unpretentious buildings.

Designing residential buildings within the Venetian fabric of canals, alleys and palaces would have been a quite different matter. Palladio's genius for innovation notwithstanding, it is hard to imagine him ignoring Venice's strong traditional typology or accepting the compromise that would eventually evolve: Despite the introduction of the classicist way, the tradition of the Gothic palace in Venice persisted. As John McAndrew remarks in his study of early Renaissance Venetian architecture:

Renaissance palaces are no bigger or showier than the preceding late Gothic ones that are equally proclamations of the glory and wealth of a family. They look different mainly because their owners wanted them to look different, and the difference is only skin-deep.[1]

On the one hand, there existed in Venice the tradition of an environmental fabric inextricably intertwined with republican society. On the other, there arrived from Rome the Renaissance search for *novitas*. In discussing the incompatibility between them, the renowned architecture critic Manfredo Tafuri compares the work of Palladio and his contemporary Jacopo Sansovino, who was a Roman expatriate practicing in Venice after the Sack of Rome by the Vandals (1527). As Tafuri points out:

the autonomous "measure" of the new *res aedificatoria* [was] entering into a difficult – perhaps impossible – dialogue with continuity, with dissolved

syntax, with the immeasurable dimension of the lagoon's urban fabric.
Sansovino would learn the difficult art of mediation, but Palladio would
impose (or would try to impose) his architectural microcosms upon a Venice
that they literally "interrupted."[2]

Surely the master builder of the Veneto would have dealt with the
Venetian context for residential buildings in his usual relaxed, but
disciplined and self-evident, manner. However successful in its
own right, would the resulting architecture have held the seductive
appeal of his villas for subsequent generations of architects?

The question remains hypothetical: we do not know that
Palladio received any such commissions. Public acceptance of a
handful of public buildings designed late in his career proved hard
enough to find. Holberton tells us:

> As it happened, during the last ten years of Palladio's life Venice had the
> opportunity to undertake its own Basilica, when the Ducal Palace was badly
> damaged by fires in 1574 and 1577. But Palladio's designs were rejected,
> and no grand gesture was made.[3]

Tafuri, in discussing the conflict between an architecture of
strong *social memory*[4] and "a discipline that pretends to found
its own programs," bluntly states Venice's dilemma *vis à vis* the
undisputed master:

> How could the proud autonomy of such a discipline be made to harmonize
> with the control exerted upon it by the magistracies and commissioners?
> How could tradition and *novitas* be made to *speak together*, without
> Venice's forfeiting the fullness of the symbolic text constituted by her
> continuity? . . . what was one to do when the "Roman" language claimed
> to be absolute? The reaction to Palladio was typical: Venice could accept
> his language, but only by pushing its propositions out to her margins – to

the Giudecca, to the island of San Giorgio, to San Francesco della Vigna, to Santa Lucia.[5]

Thus, we find an early instance of the tension, so familiar to us today, between the extant field and the vision of the individual architect. It is a troubling relationship that we have come to accept as somehow inevitable.

◉◉◉

Vitruvius Pollio was the first generalist author on architecture whose books we know. Although familiar with major Roman building innovations such as concrete vaults, he did not witness the building of the empire's greatest monuments. He wrote at the dawn of the Christian era, prior to the Coliseum in the first century AD and the Pantheon in the following century. In Vitruvius's day, the dominance of Greek architecture was waning. In summarizing what was known of the art of building, his *Ten Books on Architecture* show a marked preference for ancient Greek architecture, which Vitruvius deemed superior to what was built in his own time. The Greek architectural tradition would soon be superseded. Vitruvius, sensing a sea-change, wrote to preserve what had evolved and been perpetuated for more than a millennium.

Many centuries later, Leon Battista Alberti emulated Vitruvius. His own ten-volume compendium on the art of building similarly covers a multitude of facts and opinions, on topics that range from choosing a site to the art of lifting great weights by means of pulleys, ropes and levers.[6] In invoking the "Ancients," Alberti refers mainly to the Romans. In a society where all things Roman were studied seriously, his knowledge of their skills and works was singularly impressive. But unlike Vitruvius, Alberti's perspective was prospective. He, as well as Palladio after him, studied the

classical orders not to restore them, but to promote a way of making
architecture that was entirely new.

Alberti states his position clearly in the preface to *On the Art of
Buiding in Ten Books [De Re Aedificatoria]*:

> Him I consider the architect, who by sure and wonderful reason and
> method, knows both how to devise through his own mind and energy,
> and to realize by construction, whatever can be most beautifully fitted out
> for the noble needs of man, by the movement of weights and the joining
> and massing of bodies. To do this he must have an understanding and
> knowledge of all the highest and most noble disciplines. This then is
> the Architect.[7]

Vitruvius explains Architecture; Alberti introduces the persona of
the Architect. In Alberti's eyes, the architect, unlike the traditional
master builder, is not someone who carries on a tradition, applying
ingenuity to perpetuate and perfect it. Rather, the architect is
someone who "knows how to devise through his own mind and
energy . . . whatever can be most beautifully fitted out for the noble
needs of man."

Architecture is no longer the expression or product of a people
or of an entire culture, to which the master builder devotes a
lifetime of hands-on study. Henceforth, architecture consists of
what architects produce "by sure and wonderful reason and
method." This new definition of the architect represented a
momentous innovation. In keeping with the Age of Humanism,
Alberti's definition celebrated the architect as someone independent and capable of thinking for himself, in contrast to rule-bound
Gothic guild members.[8]

This was the time when Giorgio Vasari wrote *The Lives of the
Artists*.[9] There too, the persona came first, followed only afterward
by discussion of the work. It was also an era when merchant

client and architect were becoming equals, united by the study of classical language, history and architecture. Citizens from many walks of life shared a novel and peculiar notion: in creating things never before seen, those who possessed talent would advance the quality of the mind, the prestige of the arts and the beauty of the physical environment.

Palladio would eventually rise well above his station as a mason. But while Alberti had proposed emancipation of the architect, his purpose as an aristocrat was not necessarily to elevate masons or other craftsmen who built palaces and humble dwellings. Above all, Alberti valued ideas, art and knowledge. He most assuredly did not practice a trade. Nor did Alberti personally execute his designs; he had master craftsmen to do so for him. Alberti's redefined architect possesses a creative and educated mind. He is an inventor and organizer: a new kind of intellectual who must have knowledge, but not necessarily practical know-how. In that sense, Alberti's *On the Art of Building in Ten Books* may be understood as the compilation of all that can be learned about Architecture without actually building: it is compatible with a definition of architecture as a body of abstract knowledge.

Alberti's broad audience of patrons was comprised of humanists. In a time full of energy and new expectations, they applauded this new assertion of professional power. Ancient custom credited patrons with "building" works of renown: the emperor Hadrian "built" the Pantheon, Vespasian "built" the Coliseum. In contrast, Alberti's patron depends on the architect, a free agent, for the provision of shelter. The new relation between architect and patron stems from the notion that all that is built must be equally dependent on the Architect. For Alberti, this rests on historical fact. In the preface, following the prior quotation, we read:

> Some have said that it was fire and water which were initially responsible for bringing men together in communities, but we, considering how useful, even indispensable, a roof and walls are for men, are convinced that it was they that drew and kept men together. *We are indebted to the architect* not only for providing that safe and welcome refuge from the heat of the sun and the frosts of winter (that of itself is no small benefit), but also for his many other innovations, useful to both individuals and the public, which time and time again have so happily satisfied daily needs. [emphasis added][10]

From this general indebtedness flows the dependence of the wealthy patron as well. The prologue continues:

> How many respected families both in our own city and in others throughout the world would have totally disappeared, brought down by some temporary adversity, had not their family hearth harbored them.[11]

This amounts to "spin" that advances the new role of the architect.

As for Alberti's claim, it is neither as broad nor as general as it seems. In placing the architect on a par with his patron, it is understood that architecture as such is only to be built for the wealthy and powerful. Inevitably, in restricting the definition of the architect to intellectuals and humanists, their clientele is also defined more narrowly. The author struggles from time to time with this contradictory claim. To establish the architect as the equal of the client, the former must lay claim to knowledge of "all" building. But in serving that niche market, the majority of built environment is never considered.

Alberti similarly never seriously discusses abodes for the poor, nor even for shopkeepers or guild members. Alberti's classical authorities were invariably of Roman patrician stock. Their writings mentioned the poor only to the extent that they were useful as

servants, slaves or others attached to the master's household:
as such, they must be housed and fed by his estate. In the fifteenth
century, little of that had changed.

Roman urban fabric in its full complexity and variety would be
excavated only much later. Alberti could not know of the Rome that
existed beyond the atrium houses of the powerful. He mentions
neither the ancient multi-story tenement apartment buildings of
Ostia, nor the *tabernae*, the hole-in-the-wall shops and workplaces
above which the majority of the Roman urban population lived. More
than a millennium later, the urban fabric of Alberti's Rome still
consisted of descendants of those same typologies. Yet such buildings were not what he had in mind when discussing architecture.

How could it be otherwise? Alberti may generalize about the
role and status of the architect, so newly defined, but he is centuries
removed from the time when general statements about everyday
built environment would be seriously considered. Nor was the
seeming invisibility of urban fabric in all its complexity and sophistication a simple result of Alberti's noble upbringing or of his
fixation on the wealthy patron. The built fields of the Renaissance
were largely invisible among those who wrote and reflected
because, unlike the Greek building tradition for Vitruvius, the
implicit knowledge and way of life they embodied were not yet
endangered. That would happen only centuries later, under the
onslaught of industrialization. Throughout the intervening eras,
common urban fabric was taken for granted. It was neither
recorded, nor observed: there was simply no need to examine it.

Meanwhile, the invisibility of common fabric allowed Alberti to
pronounce the remarkable theory that the architect is the well-
spring of architecture. That belief – then so new and revolutionary
– became the foundation of our professional culture.

Todi, Italy, is renowned for its two interlocking medieval squares. One is entirely enclosed, the other looks out over the hills. A town hall marks a corner of the two overlapping squares, Todi's Gothic church stands more to the interior. Both structures are connected to the main square by monumental stairs. Both are surrounded by mundane structures that form the dense fabric of an age-old urban field out of which the squares were carved. This setting could be cited as a textbook example of the urban quality that results from a series of discrete interventions over time.

In an open field just beyond the town walls stands the Renaissance church of Santa Maria della Consolazione. A dome atop a square surrounded on all four sides by semi-circular bays beneath half-domes, its initial design is frequently attributed to Bramante.[12] The church has stood apart in self-contained symmetry since its creation.

The contrast could not be more striking: Within the town walls, a living urban fabric culminates in the juxtaposition of public spaces and buildings built in different times by different people. It forms a coherent whole; the result of a legacy of design decisions; complete, but never entirely fixed. But Santa Maria della Consolazione responds not to the town nearby, but to its own internal, complete and transparent geometry.

The buildings are also strikingly different. Nonetheless, to accurately and objectively describe the difference is difficult. Contrasting "organic" architecture vs. architecture governed by intellect and geometry, or "vernacular" vs. "formal" is too simplistic. Vernaculars such as Pompeiian houses display well-controlled symmetry and geometry as part of an urban fabric of unmistakable organic quality. Todi's Gothic church and town hall similarly exhibit intelligent design decisions and uses of geometry. The Gothic church also displays marked formality and symmetry: it

2.5 Santa Maria della Consolazione, Todi, attributed to Bramante. In this church, set within the intellectual landscape of a dispersed professional network, ancient elements are recombined to create a new architecture. Photograph © Oliver Radford, reprinted courtesy of the photographer.

would be difficult to label it "local vernacular" no matter how that term is defined.

The church at Todi – like Bramante's famous Tempietto in Rome – is a laboratory piece in which ancient elements are recombined to create a new architecture. Santa Maria della Consolazione reveals an architect who is patently disinterested in any connection with extant fabric. His architecture makes a statement intended for peers elsewhere. Architecturally, his context is not the town of Todi at all, but the intellectual landscape of a dispersed professional network of individuals, all passionately involved in a new experiment.[13]

For centuries, master builders had created buildings that extended what was there. Dimensioning and geometry figured prominently among their methodologies for relating to and extending existing context and tradition. But Bramante's generation of architects focused instead on an abstract idea: using elements found in the remains of a past culture to forge something new. In the vestiges of Roman architecture they found a self-contained geometry that was both monumental and formal, one that transcended local conditions. The Greek temple clearly suggests a similar autonomy of form. For those involved in this new way of designing, architecture was no longer a local act.

It is not difficult to recognize this attitude in modern practice. Le Corbusier's Unités d'Habitation could similarly be built anywhere, as could Mies van der Rohe's Chicago towers. At issue is not a fundamental design skill such as proper siting. Rather, it has to do with frame of reference within the architect's world, wherein acts become statements in a value system that is not local. Existing urban fabric was not only uninteresting, it was also inhibiting. Experimenting with new ideas and inventing new form and experimentation was best accomplished at arm's length. Alberti, a generation earlier than Bramante, frankly expressed this in his fifth book, *On the Works of Individuals:*

> a large number of men and things cannot be accommodated as freely in the city as they can in the country . . . In urban building there are restrictions such as party walls, dripping-gutters, public ground, rights of way, and so on, to prevent one's achieving a satisfactory result. In the countryside this does not happen.[14]

Having mentioned urban building and countryside as well as houses for the poor and the rich as all worthy of the architect's attention, Alberti announces that, in beginning his exploration of design, he will "begin with the easier. In the countryside there are fewer restrictions, and the rich are readier to invest money."[15]

This new and brutally frank rationale comes from the designer's perspective. The freestanding house preferred by the rich and powerful certainly makes design vastly easier.

But it remains a matter of preference and attitude. Mauro Codussi, a contemporary of Bramante, showed instead how the new way of working could be woven into the Venetian fabric. His church of Santa Maria Formosa adjusts its symmetry in minor but significant ways to adjacent buildings, its façades respond to the spaces it helps to shape. His Venetian *palazzi* and *scuolas* continue Gothic spatial patterns as much as they introduce Renaissance form. Although his originality and talent are beyond dispute, he simply had no qualms about tying into the extant fabric.[16]

Codussi's mastery is now widely recognized. But purists in his own time and subsequent generations of historiographers dismissed his career as one of compromise. Palladio, born four years after Codussi's death, found in Albertian rural isolation the ideal context for innovation. At the same time, as Tafuri notes, his more radical stance led Venice to keep him at arm's length. Palladio's two urban masterpieces are unlike Codussi's work: they maintain strict self-containment and do not form urban space. Their magnificent façades redefine the waterfront like stage backdrops, yet remain independent from and unaided by nearby buildings.

The Palladian stance carried the day. Unbeholden to context, it lent itself well to export. Codussi lapsed into obscurity until rescued by recent scholarship. Nevertheless, in the centuries that followed, urban fields came to accommodate and incorporate the new classicism very much in Codussi's way. "Architecture" and "vernacular" found co-existence as Palladian façades came to adorn town halls and churches throughout the world.

The issue is not purity of style, but a fundamental difference in allegiance. From now on, fields would contain what was locally cultivated in conjunction with the products of network culture.

●●●

In seventeenth-century Amsterdam, three great canals dug around the medieval urban core doubled the city's size in a single generation. The canals were built in the local manner, continuing and developing extant fabric and house typology. During the same period, the town council that supervised the creation of these canals also commissioned Jacob van Campen to build a monumental town hall at the heart of the city's medieval core. It is a glorious building, at once classical and baroque, effectively representing this rich city as the premier international commercial center it was. [Fig. 5.3]

For van Campen and his clients, the new spirit of bold invention, of Albertian ways of working, and of the interventions of Palladio and Bramante and their far-flung network, had already become part of a new social memory. This was not cultivated locally, but in a network society.

Henceforth in the urban field's physical presence and it social organization we witness the combined reflection of two fundamentally different ways. One identifies with and perpetuates local heritage, the other connects to a larger world.

●●●

The first of Alberti's ten books is *Lineamenta*. He defines that term by opposition: *Lineamenta* in architecture derives from the mind, as opposed to *materia*, which derives from nature. Alberti provides a general description of what "lineaments" do:

It is the function and duty of lineaments, then, to prescribe an appropriate place, exact numbers, a proper scale, and a graceful order for whole buildings and for each of their constituent parts, so that the whole form and appearance of the building may depend on the lineaments alone . . . It is quite possible to project whole forms in the mind without any recourse to the material, by designating and determining a fixed orientation and conjunction for the various lines and angles. Since that is the case, let lineaments be the precise and correct outline, conceived in the mind, made up of lines and angles, and perfected in the learned intellect and imagination.[17]

Over time, a variety of translations has been proposed for the term "lineamenta": *disegno, risse, form, datum lines, desire lines, schematic outlines*, etc. All have their limitations.[18] A designer is left with two impressions by this introductory passage. First, lineament is not an abstract concept, but rather a tool used by the architect to organize the building. Alberti repeatedly speaks of "lines" and "angles." Taken literally, one might envisage the geometry on which the building is based, such as a band that indicates the position and size of a pilaster, or a triangle that indicates the tympanum. This simple and reductive understanding of the term *lineamenta* may not satisfy the theorist or historiographer, but it rings true to the practicing architect. Alberti stresses the most universal aspect of building design: the spatial composition and geometric abstraction that underlie the disposition of a building's parts.

Second, Alberti places additional emphasis on the abstraction already implied by the geometry: "The building can be held in the mind without need for material information . . . Of this, the lineaments are the precise and correct outline."

These two aspects in combination introduce yet another momentous innovation: Alberti designates the domain of the architect as *design* – i.e., the abstract visualization of the building, as well as its precise proportioning and ordering principles. This

domain he separates from an entire body of tectonic knowledge –
of material properties, of the way parts are actually brought together
to resist the forces of gravity, wind, weather, etc. Design is for the
first time identified as a discrete task separate from the act of
building. As a result of this definition, a rift was created in the
seamless disciplinary memory, the body of knowledge shared by all
who made buildings.

Thus, Alberti lays the foundation of a new skill to be nurtured
by a new profession. The architect envisioned by Alberti is far more
than an intellect who has mastered all that is described in the
remaining nine books. Within a distinct discipline, the architect
is the expert when it comes to handling *lineamenta*, someone who
conceives of whole buildings entirely in the mind. This skill separates the architect from the master builder of prior generations:
the latter exercised a craft bounded by typology and custom,
material organization and construction. The former – no longer
bound to precedent and custom – is now free to create new forms
in the mind and make them come about with precision and order.

By most definitions of the term *design*, pre-Renaissance
masters designed, too. But design was extracted by Alberti as a
concept in its own right. Since the time of Alberti, there has been
little doubt that design constitutes an independent aspect or discipline; and we are convinced that it belongs to the exclusive domain
of the architect. Since that emancipation, we have also been
wrestling with a question: What is it that we actually *do* when we
design? The answers vary widely.

Isolating design as a discrete skill opened the path to what the
Renaissance most admired: innovation. Traditional architecture was
inseparably bound to extant typology. Over centuries, breathtaking
achievements – Greek temples, Gothic cathedrals, Byzantine
churches and the like – had not been invented: they evolved. They
resulted from widespread adoption of innovation in a process that

was incremental and long term. House by house and church by church, the way of building shifted little by little. Each new building involved only partial and frequently modest transformation of the type. Such incremental transformation in theme and variation contributed to collective disciplinary memory while modifying it.

Now that way was replaced by the notion that an architecture could consist of new buildings invented by freely composing a complement of parts, particularly those found in the vestiges of Roman buildings. Thus the importance of the study of ancient architecture: it provided the kit of parts of innovation. Gothic discipline could be cast off in favor of an entirely new way of making buildings. Antiquity provided not only a treasure trove of examples and ordering principles, but also authority: the aura of excellence still clung to it, together with vestigial memories of Roman grandeur. The legacy of Imperial Rome was now revived through renewed reading of its classical authors and its building remnants.

●●●

Of course, there is no such thing as a clean slate in architectural design. Human imagination cannot free itself from precedent and memory; language lives not in dictionaries, but in the mouths of others.[19] Building is no different. The act of building is furthermore bounded by the processes of production and construction. These require complex orchestration through time of many individuals possessing a variety of skills and guided by tried and true rules of thumb. Whatever coherence we do find in fields past and present is to a large extent the product of such constraints.

In that light, we admire all the more the exhilarating energy of innovation in the work of Palladio and his peers. Their writings reveal their obsession with *novitas*, our own undeniable heritage.

Throughout much of the twentieth century, the constraints of the field seemed suddenly immaterial, dwarfed by industrialization and social re-organization. Tradition broke down. Innovation became more than an artistic preference: it was a necessity. Innovation in turn seemed to require a clean slate, and the door to an ideology of the avant garde was opened: unlike the masters of the Renaissance, the moderns had no ancient authority from which to borrow.

All of this arose from a definition of architecture that compelled the profession to turn away from the field, as Bramante left Todi. Architectural theory to this day remains focused on what architects have done subsequent to that divorce. Neither Alberti's *lineamenta*, nor any mainstream design theory offered since, has connected architecture to the incremental, partial and unending process of renewal and transformation by which fields come about and are perfected over time.

About fields

THREE

Evidence of our most ancient urban fabrics is limited. Most have crumbled, destroyed by war or natural calamity, abandoned to nature or overgrown and overlaid by new and different fabrics. From the little we do know, a field, as a species, can endure for millennia. Sir Leonard Woolley's excavations of the early Mesopotamian city of Ur document a fabric of dead-end streets and courtyard houses that is clearly akin to a traditional Tunisian residential quarter documented a few decades ago. [Fig. 3.3]

Beijing has been rebuilt in its entirety several times and there is every reason to assume the houses in earlier versions of the city were of the same type. The gigantic Qianlong Era map of Beijing drawn for the emperor by French Jesuits in 1740 depicted each house, its courtyards and pavilions. [Fig. 3.1] Large parts of the same fabric persisted, albeit in a congested and deteriorated state, prior to recent large-scale demolition projects. The fabric of Venice, as we know it today, still reflects its Gothic medieval origins and many *palazzi* built at that time remain. [Figs. 2.3 and 2.4]

Transformation over time takes place in even the most constant of fields. But continuity of form and spatial organization over many generations remains the most striking quality of historic fields. John McAndrew's observation, when comparing the early Renaissance and Gothic palaces of Venice, that their difference was "only skin deep" tells us the spatial organization of the house remained constant over centuries.[1] Although the façades are

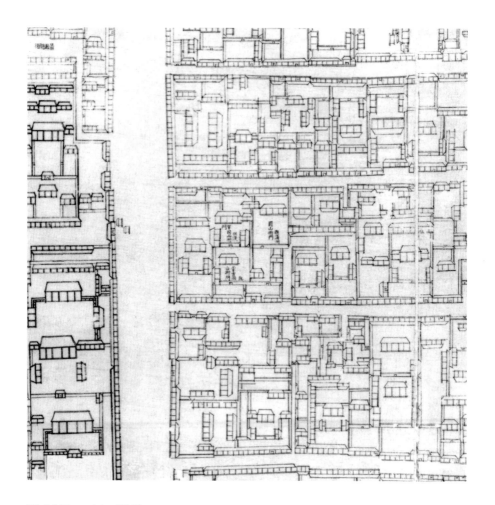

3.1–3.4 The variety of fields

3.1 Beijing. Detail photograph from the Complete Map of the Capital City during the Qianlong Era (Qianlong jingchen quantu), ca. 1750, 1935 facsimile reproduction. Typical view of the field with main street and narrow side streets. Residential compounds are reached through gates in otherwise closed walls along the side streets. The compounds contain a sequence of courtyards formed by pavilions with tiled roofs supported by wooden columns and subdivided by masonry walls. From the collection of the Harvard-Yenching Library, Harvard University. Reprinted with permission.

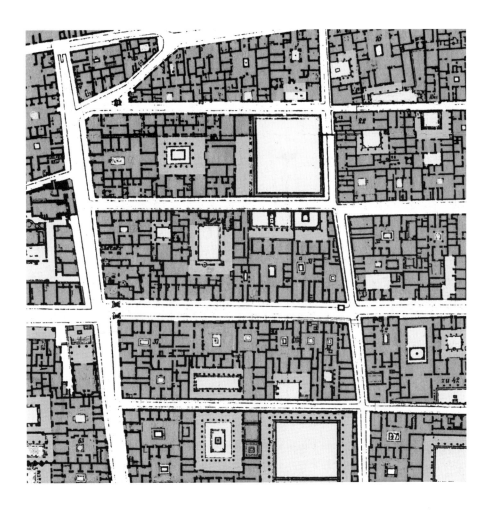

3.2 Pompeii ca. 79 AD, after a plan published by Johannes Adolf Overbeck in 1866. This sophisticated field had developed for centuries prior to being destroyed by a volcanic eruption. The plan shows instances of the house type with its sequence of spaces. A street gate provides access to the atrium which is followed by a columniated court-yard or peristyle, and sometimes by a garden. Rooms are positioned around these major spaces. Along the streets are tabernae, "hole-in-the-wall" shops and workplaces, often with living space above. Although the size of rooms is fairly constant across the field, house sizes can differ greatly, depending on the size of atrium and peristyle. Small houses frequently make do with only a partial peristyle and no garden.

3.3 Tunis Medina. Dead-end alleys lead from the major street lined with hole-in-the-wall shops to the courtyard houses. [Courtyards are shaded grey.] This ancient field, mapped when it was about to disappear, belongs to a tradition that reaches in space from Iran to Spain and in time from the city of Ur 4500 years ago [see Fig. 3.5] to the present. The Tunis Medina illustrates one of many variations on the courtyard house in that tradition. Base map courtesy of the Association Sauvegarde de la Medina, Tunis. Reprinted with permission.

3.4 Mexico City, aerial photograph ca. 1973. One of the many "informal" neighborhoods that jointly comprise the larger part of this city, a conurbation whose total number of inhabitants is now estimated to exceed 22 million. Squatters who occupy land illegally nonetheless consistently follow rules, which eventually produce a well-ordered gridded field. Within two or three decades, the resulting regular urban environment features houses that are two or three stories high, paved streets, sewers and utility systems. Eventually, entrepreneurs buy extant lots, demolish houses and erect apartment buildings. [See Fig. 3.10 and also Fig. 3.11, which depicts a local residential street 30 years after this aerial picture was taken.]

rendered in a different style, the seventeenth-century Amsterdam canal house similarly derives much of its spatial organization from its sixteenth-century precursor. While fields continuously absorb stylistic and technical change, continuity in spatial organization remains an enduring characteristic.

The emergence of fields and their growth into full bloom may take many generations as well. Our contemporary fields, many less than a century old, are just emerging and by no means fully developed.

The most striking quality of fields is the way they combine coherence and variation. Fields build and embody identity through thematic consistency. Buildings, interiors, and urban spaces in theme and variation are similar but not identical. Such coherence-in-variation suggests a property essential to the living field. Fields endure by constant transformation in a thematic manner. *Type*, *pattern*, and *system* are concepts that indicate what is constant among variants in environmental form. When complex wholes like houses or urban fabric show clear kinship, we say they are of the same *type*. *Patterns*, as defined by Christopher Alexander, imply not only a relation between parts but also the possibility of implementing that relationship differently each time.[2] Systems define parts and their relations. They are kits of parts of which many things can be made, different in shape, but similar in structure.

This vocabulary, applied with some rigor, allows us to compare the thematic qualities of fields. Renaissance client and architect may have considered themselves bold innovators, but their adventure was circumscribed. The change in Venetian fabric from Gothic to Renaissance times really amounts to a transformation of the façade as a sub-system while the overall spatial typology remains fairly constant. For that reason, we experience the Venetian fabric as a coherent whole: it is composed of parts created in different times but akin to one another.

3.5 "North Harbour" district of the City of Ur at the time of Abraham, ca. 2500 BC. Drawing by Sir Leonard Woolley *et al*, courtesy of the University of Pennsylvania Museum.

The reverse may be observed in Miami Beach's Art Deco District. There, during a short-lived and frenzied early development launched in the 1930s, architects consistently followed a prevalent fashion. The buildings exhibit strong stylistic coherence that was

3.6 Miami Beach, Florida, South Beach art deco hotel. Photograph by J. L. Teicher.

subsequently adopted in entirely different building types. In this case, the focus is on maintaining coherence and it is literally skin deep, limited to color and a few façade elements. It seems that in general spatial typology is stronger than style.

Thematic analysis allows us to describe and compare the formal qualities of fabrics. This does not explain, however, why coherence-in-variation is such a constant quality of the living field. In our contemporary condition, we assume there are always alternative ways of doing things. So why coherence?

Close examination reveals that, despite our marked architectural preference for what is new and different, today's fields are also remarkably coherent. Architects who rail against their mediocrity and the monotony sometimes fail to appreciate that coherence can be of high quality as well. In vernacular architectures throughout history, wide arrays of competing alternative themes were simply unknown. In any single locale, be it Venice or Beijing, there was one fundamental and shared way of building. In his seminal *House Form and Culture*, Amos Rapoport has argued that there always have been socio-cultural constraints. Climate, available materials, and local ways of building were constraints too, but their impact was not deterministic; it left space for cultural preference as a defining element in the thematic coherence of a field.[3]

People are born, live and die within built environment, adapting to it and translating it. The experience provides a deep and only partially explicit knowledge. More recently, the concept of social memory has denoted the constancy observed in environmental fabric over time. Environmental knowledge is not the privileged expertise of any profession, it is based on the common experience of a people. We operate within cultures that share common environmental forms. When, in the Anglo-Saxon tradition, we refer to the *attic*, *parlor*, *basement* or *porch* of a house, everyone knows what we are talking about. Our ability to discuss *squares*, *streets*, *alleys*, *lanes* and *boulevards* similarly means that the environmental spaces denoted by such terms are shared within a social body.

Attic, *basement* and *porch* do not refer to functional entities: they are architectural and spatial terms. Such *forms of understanding* – their appearance, spatial character and associations – are known to builder and lay person alike. They make environment understood and foster a tacit understanding among members of a culture. They facilitate understanding and appreciation between lay person and professional.[4]

Rooms in the traditional Japanese house are not referred to by function but by the number of tatami mats that comprise the floor.

This indication is three-dimensional; different numbers of tatami mats imply different ceiling heights. Such shared knowledge of architectural form is found in all cultures and can be very detailed.

For architects, divorced from locally shared form, understanding the inherent capacity of space to accommodate a specific function is a matter of professional expertise. Basing design on detailed program, we organize carefully metered custom space for each function, then arrange it to create architecture. Or else, we take an existing building and fit it out for client-specific program and furnishings.

Yet inhabitation is both innate and culturally ingrained. Its habits are wedded to the typological forms each culture builds and names. Social memory embedded in such forms of understanding brings professional and lay person together, leaving "function" behind.

In seventeenth-century Amsterdam, social memory underlaid the layout of the three grand canals. Lewis Mumford, an authority on cities and their transformation, rightly observes that Amsterdam's extension occurred "before it had completely dissociated itself from the customary controls and collective commitments of its medieval prototype." Yet, in referring to the Great Extension as one of the greatest examples of the town planner's art, Mumford repeatedly mentions the "plan of the the three canals." He wonders what prior urban plans might have inspired this "image on paper," and states, "The order created by the Plan of the Three Canals remained in advance of any other urban planning, taken as a whole, for three centuries."[5]

However, there was no "plan" *per se*, not in the way we use the term today. The extension was a direct continuation of the pattern of houses and canals already present in the medieval core. The town surveyor's layout was not informed by any master plan.[6] The extension repeated the pattern of concentric canals already evident in the medieval core. There was also dimensional change: the house type to be built along the canals was a variation on earlier typology, but the growing prosperity of the city allowed the house lots to be somewhat wider and considerably deeper, making large backyards possible. In contrast to the medieval canals, the new canals were dug all at once in straight sections: that scale of intervention, consistently repeated, made them monumental.[7]

In short, apart from its dimensions and regularity, the new fabric did not differ from the fabric already in place for generations. There was no consideration of alternative designs. In comparison with the agonizing and time-consuming deliberations that precede new urban extensions today, that process, already familiar for generations, was remarkably efficient. In little more than a generation, the built surface of the town doubled. It was a triumph of social memory at work.

In the nineteenth-century transformation of Parisian fabric under Napoleon III and his prefect, Baron Georges-Eugène Haussmann, we do find ample evidence of debate and controversy.[8] The project entailed a good deal of demolition, with inevitable social costs. The cutting of the Parisian boulevards through the congested medieval fabric has been denounced as a militaristic intervention intended to keep a world city under political control; it has been hailed as the beginning of the Paris that we now know; it has been seen as early evidence of modern ascendant administrative and bureaucratic power. Julian Beinart has also pointed out that perhaps the most innovative aspect of Haussmann's project was his invention of long-term borrowing to make public works feasible, a mode of operation now common worldwide.[9] Much has been made of the newness of the undertaking. Yet much remained constant, lending coherence to the monumental intervention.

There is close and obvious kinship between the courtyard buildings along the boulevards and the historic *hôtel particulier* that had been part of Parisian culture for centuries. Instances of that building type are still evident in vestiges of the historic fabric of the Île Saint-Louis, the Marais and older Left Bank neighborhoods. The house of the powerful *seigneur* or nobleman was reached via a courtyard separated from the street by a gate. Around the court, stables and service spaces were found, as well as houses for artisans and servants. The major house was located at the back, opposite the gate, between the courtyard and a private garden.

As in Amsterdam, the extant type was transformed and continued while its scale was increased. Blocks formed by the new boulevards were still filled with courtyard buildings. Workplaces were still found on the ground floor while stairs gave access to apartments on the five floors above. While the long uniform façades were of an unprecedented scale, the *French windows* and their ornate cast iron railings were familiar elements. The pattern of the *entresol* – a low floor between ground floor retail space and the apartments above – consistently seen along the boulevards is a direct continuation of traditional Parisian fabric. The entresol can be a mezzanine extension of the shop below, or it may be connected to living space above.[10]

The zone of ground floor and entresol with gates stretching full height defines the boulevard wall. Together with trees along the sidewalk, this pattern determines much of the character of Parisian life. The edges of the boulevards are alive because they are filled with retail space. This, in turn, is possible because courtyard access to the apartments makes for very deep urban blocks packed with five or six floors of residential space. Thus, courtyard, French window, and entresol work in unison to determine the very fabric of the boulevards, continuing the past in the newly built field.

The fact that social memory drove the actual building of the fabric alongside the boulevards helps to explain the rapid and

3.7 Paris, entresol-height gate leading to the courtyard of the Maison de Verre by Pierre Chareau and Bernard Bijvoet (1927-32). Photograph by J. L. Teicher.

3.8 Paris, Avenue de l'Opéra.

efficient execution of this monumental royal undertaking. No time was wasted. Alternative solutions and multiple options were not designed, compared, tested or debated. Communication among client, developer and builder was based on familiar concepts and state-of-the-art technology. Whatever regulation or control was needed could be formulated efficiently: everyone understood what was to be done in the first place. Social memory channeled the tremendous energies called forth to transform the city.

Thematic elements, once in place, can be tenacious even in times of fundamental change. But shared collective memory can also give rise to new environments of strong thematic coherence appearing on virgin soil, such as classical Greek colonies. Evidence of how, in millennia preceding ours, cities came about is to be found in the extensive so-called *informal* sectors around large cities like Mexico City, Cairo, Istanbul and Djakarta. In Mexico City, for instance, a majority of citizens have found shelter in self-help schemes, the largest of which may count more than a hundred thousand inhabitants.[11] [Fig. 3.4]

3.9 Mexico City, Colonia Santa Ursula, 1982. Early stage of a so-called "informal" settlement. Typically, squatters first build a wall around their territory with a gate (to the right of the picture) to the street. They then proceed to build within, room by room.

Once land is occupied by a social group, a grid of streets is laid out. Settlers follow carefully, building on lots determined by common consent. The consistency and coherence of the urban fabric that eventually arises are remarkable. Typologies continue traditional culture. Mexican settlers first build a wall around the lot with a gate at the street. They then proceed to build the house one room at a time, as fast as resources and energy permit. Eventually, perhaps after two decades or more, there is a large two-story house for an extended family, adjacent to similar houses, in a neighborhood that cannot be distinguished from formally subdivided fabric. In Cairo, a more dense fabric of houses several stories high, building also happens incrementally, evidenced by steel bars protruding out of the roof to reinforce future columns. Such informal processes likely produce the majority of shelter in today's world, as they had always done.[12]

Informal settlement processes are driven by a complex network of small-scale manufacturing and specialization. Small local contractors are hired. Local workshops produce tile, windows and doors of standard dimensions. These are sold to home owners piece

3.10 Mexico City, Colonia Santa Ursula, residential street, 2002. Within two or three decades, an informal settlement functions as a living and mature field.

3.11 Mexico City, Colonia Santa Ursula. Once the field has begun to mature, private capital moves in, in this case buying property and erecting an apartment building.

by piece. This entire ecology of craftsmen and traders is, in fact, fed by the global building industry. Bricks may be fired in distant yards. Cement and steel rods come from the same technically sophisticated production systems that in parallel supply the legal, formal and fully professionalized building industry. The informal sector also absorbs large quantities of sewer and water pipe, electric and data cabling and conduit, and bathroom and kitchen equipment. All of these represent products of mass manufacturing and high capital investment: the informal sector forms a market of considerable importance.

The only work never performed professionally is the actual design of the houses. Inhabitants' design decisions follow conventional patterns. Wherever groups of settlers share local background and culture, thematic coherence results.

The settlement of the American West was not much different. There too, settlers built for themselves, often helped by small local builders, carpenters and other tradesmen and unskilled laborers. Even in modest villages, timber was more often from lumber mills than from trees felled on their own land. House design was not a professional task: with the help of pattern books, settlers and builders shared a notion as to what a house was and how it ought to be built.

A dramatic example of the strong social memory shared by the settlers of the American West is found in the great Oklahoma Land Rush, as recorded by John Reps. The prairie reservations to which native Americans had been consigned were confiscated and opened up for white settlement. Would-be homesteaders could cross the state boundary on a predetermined date and hour. The ensuing rush was chaotic and fierce: "Sooners" who "jumped the gun" were followed by settlers leaping off of trains in droves, hammering stakes to mark their claim to land, and camping out that first night in open fields.[13] Yet, out of this tumult cities such as Guthrie, Oklahoma, arose. They are as gridded and coherent as any midwestern American town. Sometimes there were surveyors. Certainly there was give and take, a good deal of territorial dispute and even occasional military intervention before streets were fully agreed upon and boundaries between neighbors were settled. But the result could not have been so banal and regular without a strong shared image of what a town was all about.

The North American settler heading west and the Mexican peasant seeking subsistence in the city, like ancient Greek colonists, evidenced social memory nurtured over time and transported to a new place. Such shared memory develops over generations. But under certain circumstances, a new shared image evolves virtually overnight, producing a sudden mutation of a species of field. Several decades after the Parisian boulevards were carved, the rise of the skyscraper after the Great Chicago Fire of 1871 produced a downtown fabric of great power. This entirely new urban fabric then began to emerge across the American continent. These fields have strong thematic qualities that are not as easily explained as the continuation of something familiar. Seemingly springing out of nowhere, they have greatly impacted city form world wide ever since.

Chicago utilized the power of the grid, familiar to town building throughout the American West. But it went far beyond that. A high rise typology never before seen arose from the ashes of extant urban framework. In the history of its emergence as recorded by Carl Condit, no single profession is credited for this startling evolution in urban fabric. Engineers, architects, builders, bankers and clients participated in a shared adventure. They took advantage of the production of cast iron (and later of steel), the invention of the elevator and the development of electric power. The social memory that came into place would dominate architectural and urban thinking for generations to come.[14]

Downtown Chicago was not a vernacular field. It was the product of multi-disciplinary effort in which all building professions contributed to a whole greater than the sum of their single interventions. In retrospect, the moment of energetic innocence was short-lived. Its innovative power was lost in the wake of Daniel Burnham's self-conscious design and the 1893 Chicago World's Fair. But in that brief moment, the rebirth of Chicago demonstrated how a new social memory could develop thematically almost overnight and then persist.

As an architectural product, the urban field of Chicago has little to do with the history of Modern architecture. Louis Sullivan's Auditorium Building still stands as a masterpiece of undiminished authority. But neither Sullivan nor his draftsman Frank Lloyd Wright represents, in form or attitude, the cause of Modern architecture. As a latter-day field of great power, Chicago's Loop area was not the result of architectural invention. It energized the best of the profession to confront new conditions. In the history of architecture, the emergence of downtown fabric as we have known it for more than a century did not come from an act of volition but from a condition thrust upon the profession.

The new urban and suburban fields of the American continent did not immediately migrate to Europe. Crippled by World War I and its resulting social and economic chaos, weighed down by historic urban fabric and related social memories, Europe's professional attempts remained tentative and fragmented, and their development was limited and quickly arrested. Berlage's extension of Amsterdam provided the context that gave rise to the famous Amsterdam School of architecture. [Fig. 4.3] It is a demonstration of peer group cooperation among architects motivated by a shared idealism. We can admire the skillful design of façades the size of an urban block and the dexterous detailing of brick, carpentry and tile. But in retrospect, we find its social memory restricted to a professional class of architects, backed by housing administrators, builders and developers, all seemingly catering to the preferences of those who controlled the flow of public funds. The actual inhabitants remained without voice.

An equally admirable Modernist neighborhood was built in Palestine under the aegis of the British protectorate by early Jewish settlers. Set on the slope of Haifa's Mount Carmel, the modernist architecture of concrete and glass structures with rounded balconies and bay windows was inspired by Eric Mendelsohn's architecture and realized in a consistent and poetic manner. Yet here too no lasting shared memory developed. Concrete was championed by the Jewish settlers not only to suggest a liberation from the past, but also to break the monopoly of local Arab inhabitants who owned the stone quarries. But subsequent settlers did not share similar preferences.[15]

Similarly, Art Nouveau aspired to a new environmental quality reflecting a spirit of invention and renewal combined with arts and crafts production. But it, too, was predominantly a stylistic movement embraced by designers and clients who longed for renewal. In all of these examples, a professional class of designers, their clients,

3.12 Old Haifa. Originally a pre-war Jewish settlement under the British protectorate, Haifa's architecture was inspired both by Eric Mendelsohn and by Bauhaus principles.

administrators and backers, no longer rooted in the broader build-ing culture, embodied their hopes and preferences in movements that were inevitably short-lived, regardless of artistic merit.

In the wake of World War II, destruction, neglect and demo-graphic trends, accompanied by developments in logistics, brought large-scale residential construction throughout the world. Entirely different developments arose in Japan, Europe and the North American continent. In America, suburban life, already in ascent prior to the war, rapidly became the norm. This trend dominated both rural and urban residential culture in terms of sheer expan-sion, demographic weight and normative impact. This new variety of field displayed specific characteristics that were largely implicit yet understood and sustained by builders, developers, politicians and inhabitants alike, in true vernacular tradition. [Fig. 4.2] Although varied house types came about, all serving the ambitions and hopes of the nuclear family of the industrial age, a common way of building – somewhat without regard to climate or landscape –

3.13 Austin, Texas, freestanding single-family bungalow, ca. 1927. Austin's Hyde Park neighborhood, was the first streetcar suburb north of the city.

contributed to suburbia's efficient production. Typical in post-war America were open lawns without walls or fences, a pattern that provides the illusion of living in the open plains without constraints, free from danger.

We are hard pressed to find historical precedents for fields, urban or suburban, in which territory is not walled or fenced-in and securely gated. Perhaps the Palladian villa comes closest to that image. And surely the Albertian preference for the freedom obtained by building outside the city can be recognized. But it must have been the "motor car" combined with a genuine sense of freedom and security, rather than any specific architectural ideology from European historic stock, that spawned such environment. All parties shared a similar image of the suburban field. Its emergence followed the age-old vernacular manner, and the mainstream of the architecture profession remained on the fringe of this movement for many decades. Like Palladio in Venice, architects were both unwilling to participate and uninvited. To the extent that professional designers were involved in producing and conceiving the everyday suburban house, they operated outside architectural history; neither recognized by their peers as contributors to an architectural tradition, nor claiming such recognition for themselves.[16]

In post-war Japan, fragmented land ownership led to a continuation of small-scale residential construction. No new varieties of fields came about at first. Instead, Japan witnessed the transformation and proliferation of extant fabric. This included the introduction of cooperative apartment buildings built upon consolidated private lots, as well as tall buildings on narrow lots in the big cities. Because Japan lacked available open space, large housing estates in the European manner or vast suburban fields in the American way were impossible. Nor did the Japanese dweller aspire to such foreign models. Innovation was mainly geared towards a more efficiently produced and better equipped free-standing house that could be custom-designed and built quickly. Industrial production was harnessed toward that end in various ways. Old ways of working were streamlined and new technical systems were developed. Mills embraced numerically-controlled production and the nascent computer to quickly produce traditionally detailed timber frame components and joinery. The frames were then assembled on-site in the age-old manner by local craftsmen. In most cases, the frames were designed as an open system to accept a variety of off-the-shelf products and subsystems.

Focus on the free-standing custom-designed house led to innovations in design and production processes. To design each house in response to client preferences, large companies began to offer local design services via dealer networks. Design was supported by computer-aided cost calculation, production of drawings and manufacturing. At the height of the Japanese real estate boom, the Sekisui company sold 60,000 custom houses a year throughout the nation.[17] This represented a new process broadly applied to the ongoing piecemeal transformation of the fine-grained living fabric. Having gone beyond Albertian ideology, a professional class brought extant fields to the threshold of a new age by systematizing in service of fine-grained fabric. As a result, Japanese residential fields, by and large maintained, by gradual transformation, a social memory shared by all sectors of the society, professional and otherwise.

In contrast, there emerged in Europe in the period between the two world wars an entirely new kind of environmental approach: mass housing. As a fundamental point of departure, the professionals involved believed the housing conditions of the urban masses could only be improved by a well-coordinated and centralized effort to produce shelter for them on a massive scale. The process provided for no thematic variety of form. Instead, there were identical floor plans in identical apartment blocks standing in rows in open fields. It is important to note that this pathology did not result from industrial production, but from an ideologically-based rejection of fine-grained processes. During this era of increasing centralization and concentration of power, it seemed somehow natural for financial and political decisions to become centralized and for control of environmental form to be placed firmly into hands those in charge could trust. Design was therefore awarded to professionals controlled by professionals. Occupancy of subsidized units was every bit as controlled as design and building. Fine-grained transformation in response to life, itself, was effectively excluded. [Figs 7.1 and 7.2]

In Europe, highly institutionalized mass housing continued through most of the twentieth century. Extending into the vast Russian steppes, it sheltered perhaps a hundred million Europeans.

3.14 Island of Mykonos, Greece. Many little private churches of a similar type are scattered throughout the countryside.

Mass housing did not evolve out of historical ways of building. Nor did it embody universal cultural understanding. Such vast stretches of real estate, characterized as they are by the extraordinarily coarse fabric that is characteristic of large-scale top-down control, are unable to transform or renew themselves unless by wholesale renovation. They cannot properly be called fields.

●●●

Fields – and the knowledge of fields – are the framework within which Architecture, the self-conscious building that deliberately transcends the thematic, occurs. In that sense, the Gothic cathedral is Architecture while Gothic houses in the fields surrounding the cathedral in theme and variation are not. Yet the cathedral arises from the everyday buildings of the field as a flower buds among the

leaves of the tree. [Fig. 5.2] The relationship between Architecture
– the special building– and the field can be very close or almost
entirely independent. The special building can result from highly
specialized design or building technology not found in the broader
field. But the special can also be constructed by the builders of the
common house. Its spatial organization can parallel or sharply
contrast the typology common to the field. In all such cases, however, we find meaning in the relation of the two, and an expression
of the culture of the age.

●●●

The churches on the island of Mykonos are scattered over the hill-
sides, freestanding white and vaulted volumes. One wall rises above
the tiled roof and holds a bell. Although sited apart from the clus-
tered villages and farm compounds, their thematic unity with the
broader fabric exemplifies the special as a thematic transformation
remaining close to the source.

Another example of thematic closeness of the special building
is found in Ming era temples depicted throughout the Qianlong Era
Map of Beijing. These are so similar in plan to the courtyard houses
that surround them that we cannot identify them by shape, only by
names written in the map. In both examples, the builders clearly
came from the field itself, although in Beijing the best craftsmen and
designers were elevated to specialize in the making of temples and
palaces. This is true as well at Katsura Imperial Palace outside of
Kyoto. There, the sophistication – including the deliberate "ordinar-
iness" of its fine details – betrays the eye and hand of master builders,
while remaining very close to traditional vernacular building.

The Old Church in Amsterdam is very different in size from the
houses surrounding it. [Fig. 5.2] Built in the Gothic tradition, its
many bays are residential-sized in plan but monumental in height.

3.15 Katsura Imperial Villa, Kyoto, Japan. From left to right: the new palace, musical instruments room and middle shoin. Together with the old shoin (further right and off-camera), this forms the main building, proper.

The church's history is one of continuous transformation and growth over several centuries. Cobbled together phase after phase, its craftsmanship closely resembles that of the residential vernacular. The result of the successive interventions is a noble space that is thematic in its variations from bay to bay, but more easily conceived of as organically grown than as the result of premeditated design. The building transcends the local themes from which it grew. But for all of its monumental presence, the Old Church remains very much a product of its native field.

●━●━●

After Palladio, there still remained architects of repute closely engaged in the field. In the late seventeenth century, along the canals of Amsterdam, houses designed by signature architects displace the works of master builders of old. They display familiarity with international stylistic principles but remain very close to the ongoing typology. There is no wholesale attempt to violate the system.

As a consequence, architectural innovation remains embedded in extant social memory, shared between client and architect. The relationship is venerable. We can similarly find late Pompeiian houses in which the design, influenced by the fashion of Rome, grafted Roman preferences onto the local way of building. Innovation is a constant human impulse. But it need not contradict extant themes.

Palladio himself used thematic elements with great sophistication. As noted previously, the columniated portico was found throughout medieval Padua and the small square cornice windows of his façades were borrowed from local farmhouse building. It should therefore come as no surprise that, in the centuries after Palladio, architects of great repute continued to operate in a deliberately thematic way. Robert Adams's London townhouses are full of invention and new neo-classical vocabulary elements. These delightful variations on an extant type in no way challenge the prevailing spatial order. And for good reason: the London townhouse had evolved through successive generations exploring the uses of a narrow site with light from front and back only. Even a "maverick" like Antoni Gaudí, in his famous Pedrera building set in the nineteenth-century Barcelona fabric, abided by traditional features of the large urban house: the entryway open to horse and carriage, monumental stairs leading up to the main floor; courtyards lending light to all floors; basement floor containing shops and workplaces open to the street with the principal floor above; glass-paned windows with shutters to bring shade; and sizable balconies. These thematic elements reinforce rather than diminish Gaudí's daring forms, and render Pedrera's façade, its roofscapes and the undulating plasticity of its interior spaces comprehensible.

There is also widespread historic evidence of architecture with scant thematic relation to the surrounding field, such as van Campen's monumental Amsterdam town hall. That building, executed in the classical manner, has little or no typological or stylistic connection to its medieval context. It was a deliberate strategy: the town hall identified Amsterdam as a world city, the center of a commercial network stretching from Japan to the Americas. Canal house architecture was built upon extant social memory, the town hall expressed the values of an international elite. In a similar way, North American town halls and court houses obey the compositional canons of a far-flung neo-classical network and display impeccable proportions, while the skillful realization of wooden columns and pediment is solidly embedded in the local vernacular of clapboard houses and barns. Such co-existence made it possible for the Palladian tradition to transcend national boundaries.

●●●

The historic relation between Architecture and the field in all its varied manifestations was self-evident, immediate and familiar. So much so that the very existence of fields did not register in architectural thinking. The Modernist era was the first in history where the dialogue between field and architecture was disrupted. New technology, new materials and new scales of intervention rendered traditional building crafts and familiar typology obsolete.

Everyday environment could no longer be taken for granted. But this was not viewed as a loss: in the Modernist perspective, the obsolete technology and typology of historic environment rendered it irrelevant, a hindrance. The self-structuring, self-repairing and self-sustaining everyday environment had proved inadequate to the task of providing housing for a burgeoning population. The emergence of common shelter was redefined: henceforth, it was a commodity to be provided.

Everyday environment became a professional design problem, to be solved through Albertian innovation. Thus, architecture undertook to reinvent the common fabric that had bound cultures for millennia.

From now on, all that was built could be Architecture.

Encounters with the field   FOUR

The most comprehensive early modern attempt to design ordinary environment was Tony Garnier's *Une Cité Industrielle: Étude pour la Construction des Villes.*[1] Begun at the turn of the twentieth century, Garnier's drawings propose a fully conceived and exquisitely rendered environment for modern society. There are public buildings, transportation systems, factories, sports facilities, schools and residential neighborhoods. The design depicts turn of the twentieth-century expectations for the future – the dynamics of bustling crowds and large public buildings. It also predicts the domestic affluence and calm of modest urban villas and of apartment buildings of equally modest size, sited in communal gardens with walkways shaded by trees and lined with shrubs. Flower beds blend with porches and sculpture.

There is no proletariat environment in the *Cité Industrielle*. All is blissful, all is bourgeois. A century later, the environment proposed by Garnier is remarkable not so much for the dynamics of modernity it sought to give shape to, as for the humanity of its spaces and its careful attention to detail. It is also steeped in the nineteenth-century Romantic tradition: the city is sited in a pastoral, mountainous and otherwise uninhabited landscape.

The seductive quality and eminent humanity of Garnier's proposals convinced his contemporaries that architects could harness and control the frightful powers of production unleashed in the age of Modernity. Good intentions and talent would prevail.

4.1–4.2 The field as a professional product

4.1 Residential neighborhood in Tony Garnier's *Une Cité Industrielle*. This 1917 proposal was one of the first professionally designed fields. It displays characteristics typical of most similar initiatives in the century that followed.

4.2 San Francisco Bay Area, Daly City, 1972. Urban layout, house design and construction betray a single hand, blurring the distinction between urban and architectural intervention in this post-war field. Despite questionable design at several scales, this field nevertheless respects traditional individual ownership and territorial boundaries: it may, with luck and time, evolve in something more viable, or else simply wither away.

4.3 H. P. Berlage's Extension of Amsterdam, 1916. Berlage's urban concept provided the backdrop for development of the famous "Amsterdam School" architecture of the 1920s and 1930s, at a point of transition toward modernist urban design and architecture. While Amsterdam South presented a professionally designed and developed environment, it nevertheless still proposed urban space as a structuring device and employed traditional craftsmanship in the execution of its innovative facades. Participating architects shared a common desire to make a successful whole, and were consequently ready to cooperate and accept peer group oversight and coordination.

4.4 Extension of Amsterdam ca. 1960. Following the second world war, urban space no longer structures the plan, which is now dominated by free-standing blocks. The urban designer now forms a plan by distributing such blocks, blurring the distinction between urban design and architecture. Photograph © KLM Aerocarto NL. Reprinted with permission.

They could bring design within reach of all classes. They would create not only public facilities for education, sports, the arts and transportation, but also a domestic affluence hitherto accessible to few. Good design could render the world good.

The isolation in which Garnier's design of the *Cité Industrielle* came about is striking. It is also telling. After years spent in an atelier while attending the École des Beaux Arts in Paris, Garnier was awarded the school's prestigious Grand Prix de Rome. Next we see him sequestered for years in Rome, designing the future. Later, he expanded his plans for that ideal environment while simultaneously building a solid professional practice in the provincial French city of Lyon.[2] Garnier required neither counsel nor stimulation from peers. He worked without an axe to grind or a manifesto to disseminate. He applied the skills acquired at the Beaux Arts effortlessly while ignoring that school's traditions and expectations.

When in Rome, Garnier did not focus on a single monumental ancient building as expected. Instead, he chose as his subject an urban fabric, the remains of an entire Roman provincial town near present-day Frascati. In his rendered general plan of Tusculum, Garnier depicted an urban environment detailed down to the furniture in the individual rooms and the pavement of the streets and squares.[3] Attracted by the wholeness of his subject, he must have sensed that in it lay the roots of the culture of the ancients that also brought forth their monumental architecture. Having studied the ancient fabric, he courageously set out to create a fabric for his own times. Garnier rightly sensed that this was the real challenge to be confronted. But if he was a pioneer in that inevitable direction, he also was among the first to act on the mistaken notion that the modernist challenge could be met by masterful architectural design in the Palladian tradition.

Palladio, in his own search to replace the "barbarism" of his times, had returned to the work of the ancients, including an extended study tour in Rome. Several centuries later, Garnier again sought to restore a link to age-old values, to again demonstrate how timeless Mediterranean well-being could inoculate the contemporary environment, this time against the malaise of industrialization. This is particularly evident in his residential proposals. Their serenity, comprehensiveness and meticulous detailing suggest that the transition from monumental Architecture to the creation of everyday environment really raises no particular questions. It is fundamentally all a matter of good design. His work made the shift look entirely within the grasp of any talented designer.

Garnier's *Cité Industrielle* heralded many developments typical of the modern. His detailed architectural rendering of what was, in scale and comprehensiveness, an urban proposal, entirely obscured the boundary between the urban level of intervention and that of architecture. While there is hierarchical order in what he proposes, there is no recognition that such hierarchy implies different parties intervening on different levels. The same practiced hand treats all elements at all scales simultaneously and with equally detailed attention. This suggested a continuum of intervention and introduced the canon of centralized design still seen as a professional ideal: the belief that a single designer should be in control of all levels of environmental form. It presaged Mies van der Rohe's simultaneous creation of both the skyscraper and the chair placed in its lobby.

Garnier's orderly and humane approach also initiated a tradition of urbanism that expresses fundamentally suburban values. Garnier shared Alberti's preference for the free-standing building as the ideal subject for architectural articulation. The idea of the city as a distribution of free-standing "villas" – very different in size and function, but always self-contained – was subsequently articulated by the Garden Cities movement. Albertian escape from the compact field combined easily with the introduction of streetcar and automobile. It became mainstream urbanism.

Garnier's residential environment also presaged contemporary (sub)urbanism in its complete lack of territorial demarcation. As in post-war suburbia in the United States, there are neither fences, nor any other physical markers of the boundary between public and private space. Nor are there backyards. Well-manicured lawns and plantings surround buildings on all sides, stretching from back of house to back of house just as they extend from sidewalk to main entry. People stroll along in pairs, as oblivious of any territorial reality as the architect who rendered them. [Fig. 4.1] The ultimate expression of such ignorance in Le Corbusier's poetic rendering of Unités d'Habitation hovering over immaculate lawns would subsequently set a vision and a precedent for generations of architects.

Garnier's overall legacy was the idea of the city as a massive, intricately crafted architectural work of art. This powerful vision further enhanced the architectural profession's singular obsession with perfecting form and crafting it down to the last detail. Within the evolving culture of architecture, this path led to a preference for form as novelty over form as a common good, for clever solutions over sustained development and for bold imagination over thoughtful questions. The future of built environment had become a matter of brilliant all-encompassing vision rather than patient cultivation. Henceforth, in the eyes of the designer, key forces that shaped the daily emergence of ordinary fabric – money, technology, demography, culture, history and popular preference – would not be trusted. Where they could not be exorcised, they would be guided by good design.

The inheritors of Garnier lacked his serene confidence. Their proposals took the form of manifestos, protests, fantasies and acts of self-promotion: Le Corbusier, in his early writings and in his Plan Voisin, rejected the historic city in a singularly and deliberately brutal gesture.[4] Frank Lloyd Wright's Broadacre City turned away from the industrial city to assert the car culture of the great

American plains. Metabolist megastructures celebrated the dynamics of movement and change. Kenzo Tange shifted to a yet larger scale, proposing the creation of artificial hills on reclaimed land in Tokyo Bay. Like others in Europe, Yona Friedman saw in small-scale human settlement an opportunity to create transparent urban mega-structures. These dreams were all in line with the Albertian notion of the architect "who by sure and wonderful reason and method, knows both how to devise through his own mind and energy, and to realize by construction, whatever can be most beautifully fitted out for the noble needs of man."

The architect's role during the massive upheavals of modern times is often cast in the perspective of a courageous avant garde. Certainly, in the early twentieth century, courage *was* displayed in many initiatives. But it was the courage of the uprooted. At the time, the massive ongoing changes in built environment must have made the world appear out of control. Against this backdrop, the best and the brightest talents of the architectural profession, aware of what was going on, came to reject both past and present as they desperately sought to maintain self-respect and artistic integrity.

This created stylistic purism, free of precedent. It also inevitably called forth a new conceptual framework to support design decisions. Demographic pressure had turned the tightly integrated traditional fabric of European cities into an unworkable mess. CIAM (Congrès Internationaux d'Architecture Moderne), in its declarations and manifestos, sought to hammer out an architectural ideology that would allow alignment with the powers that shape environment. A new formulation of distinct functional concepts – transportation, work, habitation and recreation – was adopted to help sort it out. Functional distinctions were taken literally, leading designers to separate them in time and space. In practice, this helped designers to "do their own thing" without too much interaction with others. They also paid little attention to what might be shared beyond utility lines. Buildings stood free in isolated space, streets and squares were displaced to make way for various modes of transportation. This functionalist notion was all the more potent because, thanks to cars, trolleys, commuter rail lines and, above all, the unlimited availability of land, suburban America was already building what CIAM sought to invent in the abstract.

In Europe, the majority of architects subscribed to Modernism only after the war. At the same time, they became involved in designing everyday environment. Combatant armies had destroyed much. But war had also demonstrated the power of logistics. It was possible to manage war machines of awesome power, to equip millions of soldiers and move them across the globe. Surely this unprecedented ability to produce and organize could be redirected toward the creation of new cities and a new architecture. In that instant, the geometric clarity of Modernist design seemed to match the enticing magnitude of post-war rebuilding.

In the 1950s and early 1960s, even mediocre architects were inspired by a mounting sense of power. For more than a century, science, medicine, agriculture, manufacturing and engineering had been building global professional institutions. Now these professions were joined by logisticians and managers, newer disciplines tested in wartime. All shared the architect's belief in a future that could be designed.

Looking back, we can see in that post-war era a sincere and concerted attempt by the professions to replace losses throughout the post-war world and create everyday environment on a massive scale. We can also see the Palladian attitude at work. Cornelis van Eesteren's extension of Amsterdam, with its distribution of free-standing high-rise blocks, was internationally hailed as a demonstration of CIAM principles, an example of the city of the future. [Fig. 4.4] Lucio Costa's freehand sketches for Brazilia embodied the romantic notion that great ideas by gifted individuals could make a metropolis take shape upon a desolate plain. Oscar Niemeyer's enlarged doodles confirmed the primacy of inspiration in the solution of large projects in Brazilia. In India, Le Corbusier's Chandigarh asserted that an urban and governmental center could be a one-man show of inspired sculptural buildings. Stimulated by such great examples, architects as well as students proposed dream cities, convinced that before long these too would be made real.

Great expectations were mixed with a sense of mission. In the 1950s, faculty and practicing architects in seminars or studio never missed an opportunity to testify to their concern for humanity, for a better environment: We, the architects of the world, had to invent it from scratch. Once created, we would then be responsible for it. It was a time when a renowned member of the faculty at Delft – admittedly a man at once easily excited and prone to exaggeration – proclaimed that only if we succeeded in designing the right cities might a third world war be avoided. No one laughed.

That sense of mission, albeit at times hypocritical and self-serving, was mostly genuine. As architects, we believed ourselves to be responsible for the future of environment, hence of humankind. Mass housing was designed with the sincere intent of improving conditions for the common folk. When such commissions were passionately sought, it was not solely because of their enormous construction value and profitability. Passion was further stimulated by a profound sense of paternalism shared among many professions in the post-war era – and by the unprecedented social importance and scale of the work.

The conception and production of environment became a multi-disciplinary affair. There was no place for inhabitants or other ordinary citizens in place-making: they were effectively removed from the process. As for the architects, our earnest involvement only exposed the limits of our influence. While all agreed, fatefully, that centralized control of environmental production was inevitable, responsibility was ill-defined and subject to consensus among professionals. The emerging process rewarded neither individual good intentions, nor calls for reflection.

Blame it on bureaucracy, technology, commerce or architectural dreaming: over time the professions drifted away from a shared sense of mission. Each discipline asserted itself with increasing self-interest. By the end of the 1960s, the dialogue among architects still reflected a desire for better environment, but without high hopes for imminent success. Rebelling students denounced old convictions and faded sentiments as naïve and hypocritical, betraying ignorance of the dangers of mass industrialization. The social dispute grew increasingly politicized and rancorous. Before long, architects who tried to just follow their calling shied away from social purpose: they simply wanted to make good architecture. But it was no longer simple.

●●●

Years of doubt and re-assessment ensued. Discourse and writing on architecture of that era reveal attempts to find a fresh perspective. But most of what was considered theory of architecture had to do with the architect's identity: explaining our role, bolstering our waning prestige, or reinforcing our domain. Robert Venturi's *Complexity and Contradiction in Architecture*[5] did not discuss environmental complexity or thematic contradiction. Bolstered by historical evidence, Venturi argued that it was alright for an architect to be idiosyncratic. The book's enthusiastic acceptance underscored the profession's desire to be freed from Modernity's ideology.

Steen Eiler Rasmussen's *Experiencing Architecture*[6] bypassed Modernist dogma to sensitize generations of architects to the way architectural form affects human life and perception. Rasmussen provided a wealth of significant observations and taught countless practitioners to observe environmental form in relation to human life. But implicitly, his message followed Garnier's: good environment is primarily a matter of design, a work of art.

Venturi's and Rasmussen's writings indicate the gulf between the architect and the field. Urban fabric as something discrete, beautiful and inspiring had already been "discovered" by the profession in the nineteenth century. But it remained marginal to the quest for a new architecture. Prior to Tony Garnier, Camillo Sitte had called attention to the qualities of medieval urban fields, and his writing had garnered wide interest. But Sitte's morphological approach gave little recognition to medieval fabric as the product of an entire culture – as opposed to an aesthetic preference – the technological and social values of which could not be separated. Sitte's position continued to find adherents, eventually resonating in the work of Rob Krier.[7]

Neither the thematic continuity of fields, nor their compatibility with social structure, nor their ability to inspire architecture was considered in the post-modern re-evaluation of the architect's role. Although Colin Rowe did recognize an extended fabric, his preoccupation with the autonomous architectural act prevailed throughout *Collage City*.[8] In advocating inspired improvisation, Rowe's innovation was to point out that environment was not cast from one mold but could be seen as an accumulation of successive architectural interventions. This touched on the idea of environment as a result of dialogue or of accumulation over time, and in so doing it contradicted modernist ideology and design proposals. However, collage interplay did not point the way toward the study of fields. Nor did it lead to a critique of thematic consistency. Rather, it reinforced the designer's artistic monologue.

Aldo Rossi's *The Architecture of the City*,[9] on the other hand, showed full awareness of the continuity and structure of urban fabric in which he found architectural inspiration. But Rossi did not dwell on the dynamic behavior of fields or their hierarchical structure. His recognition of urban fabric as a source of inspiration in some ways represented a return to neo-classical times, with the architect as a cognizant but staunchly independent agent. Rossi popularized the notion of typology, but neither as a source of coherence, nor as a product of social convention. Urban fabric was, in his view, at best an inspiring context. Living fabric as a nourishing force imposing its own ways remained unexamined. Nevertheless, Rossi's work made succeeding generations aware of extant urban fabric, and taught them to treat it with respect and affinity.

Earlier, Saverio Muratori and those who furthered his research had argued that urban fabric was more than an inspiring context. They recognized architectural and urban form as the product of an entire culture and advocated for painstaking examination of historical precedence. They further saw that typology was central to that cultural process. Muratori defined type as an *a priori* synthesis. In the building type, he saw "what springs to the mind of designers as the spontaneous cultural outgrowth of their backgrounds . . . deeply rooted in collective unconsciousness."[10]

The hope of Muratori and his followers was to extrapolate and project from local typology an architecture consistent with contemporary life. Unfortunately, although they sought general principles, their love of Italian fabric was exclusive. It led neither to comparative studies nor to a methodology by which to conduct such comparison. They did not convincingly succeed in separating specific values embodied in the Italian fields from the broad thematic and structural principles that govern all fields. But, to their lasting credit, they were among the first to confront the divide that separates contemporary practice from the lessons of the historic field.

In all, the works cited above did sensitize architects to extant fabric, and therefore built the foundation that supported a later generation's efforts to contribute to the renewal and upgrading of inner cities, stimulating thematic behavior in an age-old implicit way. Where strong and mature fabric was already in place, the post-war neglect of extant historic fabrics was in many cases turned around.

Yet it fell to Robert Venturi in collaboration with Denise Scott Brown and Stephen Izenour to confront mainstream architecture with the living field.[11] *Learning from Las Vegas* was not interested in typological or other structural qualities underneath the exuberant forms of Las Vegas. Yet its authors did recognize the Las Vegas fabric as an autonomous and spontaneous contemporary vernacular, an exotic species that was neither premeditated nor invented by architects. Venturi *et al.* had the further temerity to suggest that architects might learn from it.

This was the moral equivalent of positing in Victorian society that man had descended from the apes. Among architects, it heralded a massive commotion comparable to that occasioned by Darwin's theory of evolution. In the end, the professional mainstream decided not so much to study and learn, as to appropriate with artistic license. Discovering a new well-spring of artistic inspiration seemed sufficient. Subsequently, architects have felt free to borrow from the vernacular and vulgar as much as from the formal and monumental.

Bound to a profession whose sensibilities had effectively obscured the urban field, architects lacked both the botanist's open and non-judgmental fascination with all species, and his or her commitment to cultivate them without preference. Those who did advocate for the field frequently became alienated or ostracized from the mainstream.

John Turner's investigations of the squatter fields of Lima, Peru, revealed that fields, more often than not, did emerge and come to full bloom with no professional help whatsoever. The

self-organizing process by which they came about simply did not
need professional design intervention: it needed to be nourished
with materials and stimulated with economic opportunity. [Figs 3.4
and 3.9–3.11] Turner advocated a new kind of professionalism in
support of informal processes in developing countries.[12] His
writings represent a first sustained and critical attempt to draw
professional consequences from the autonomy of fields. When the
message of Turner's collaboration with Horatio Caminos of MIT
was finally heeded, it was the World Bank, not prestigious design
firms, who listened to and employed Caminos's students.

What Turner found in squatter housing in Peru, Jane Jacobs
found in the living fabric of New York City. *The Death and Life of
Great American Cities* acquired cult status. In it, Jacobs portrayed
New York as a living and autonomous fabric defying all attempts to
harness it. Her advocacy of the diversity of urban life was
unabashed. It exposed the inadequacy of functionalist thinking
and idealistic utopian visions and theories alike. Her book did
not advance a theory. Rather, it simply and powerfully observed a
mega-city animated by the forces of life in defiance of all attempts
to subject it to "design."

Jacobs displayed an unshakable trust in the workings of everyday life. Delightfully opinionated and pragmatic, well informed
about the influences of money, politics and power and dismissive of
authority and theory, she stated that "to approach a city . . . as if it
were a larger architectural problem . . . is to make the mistake of
attempting to substitute art for life."[13] This and similar pronounce-
ments led generations of students to see that urban fields like New
York are too diverse and too animated to be designed. But neither
Jacobs nor her architect admirers pursued that truism to its logical
consequences. The art vs. life debate dates back to the emancipation
of the artist in Palladian times. Acceptance of the very distinction is
a product of that emancipation and obscures the deeper dilemma

from which it arises. As a direct result, any discussion of the profession's re-entry into the field was precluded.

Christopher Alexander established the concept of patterns and suggested that a "pattern language" could be observed at work in healthy built environment. He catalogued many patterns at length, in an attempt to objectively demonstrate their validity. He argued that architects needed to understand those patterns and work with them.[14] His work was simultaneously denounced as romantic and impractical and dogmatic by researchers and critics. There were qualms about the inherent subjectivity of Alexander's patterns. There was also skepticism that patterns could provide a "turnkey" solution for matching design to life. But Alexander's great unspoken sin was to propose rigor and discipline in a new guise to a generation caught up in freeing itself from bondage to Modernism.

None of this diminishes the importance of Christopher Alexander's seminal point: built environment has its own structuring elements, and they are independent of architects' preferences and inventions. Alexander further proposed a method for finding, describing and working with patterns, instinctively coupling design themes with methods.

●━●━●

It was while all of this was taking place that I first proposed the separation of "support" and "infill" in mass housing to allow inhabitants to design their own houses within an architectural infrastructure. The stance was not political but existential: an attempt to restore a fine-grained living field. This was not advocacy of "participation" – as was fashionable in those days – but a proposal to somehow re-introduce the timeless "natural relation" between inhabitation and environment in a contemporary context. Like Turner and Alexander, I recognized the field's autonomy and sought to define a new role for a profession in harmony with it. Subsequent research led to the creation of methodological tools for architects to work in this more dynamic way. Decades later, these so-called "supports" principles, within a new sustainable approach to the design, financing, construction and life cycle inhabitation of dwellings known as *open building*, have emerged throughout the globe. Worldwide, projects have been constructed according to supports principles, articles, research reports and books on the topic have been published. Open building has been formally endorsed by some governments. Yet it remains far removed from the mainstream of architectural theory and criticism.

Recently, the New Urbanist movement, at the instigation of Andrés Duany, Elizabeth Plater-Zyberk, Peter Calthorpe and others, has called attention to suburban environment. Initially advocating a certain stylistic coherence, higher density and a pedestrian-oriented fabric, the movement became multi-faceted as it attracted a growing number of professionals. It amounts to a fairly wide-spread examination of North American suburbia. But quite apart from its advocacy, New Urbanism must be understood as a profession's long-overdue recognition, for better and for worse, of suburbia's existence. It represents a serious mainstream professional commitment to an everyday species of field long neglected by architectural thinking and discounted as a subject fit for serious architectural involvement.

It is too early to say what the recognition of fields will mean for a new academic or professional discipline. But we may expect a fresh perception that focuses on what is shared and constant across a given terrain. *Suburban Space*, Renée Chow's recent study of American suburbia as a continuity of form and space, demonstrates the possibility of a field-oriented perspective; it makes us see in an entirely new way what had perhaps become too familiar to be noted.[15]

●●●

Our current relationship to everyday environment, while clinging to the Palladian self-image, produces a peculiar dilemma. To architects prepared to design buildings for any purpose, anything built *can be* architecture. On the other hand, not everything necessarily *is* architecture: to claim otherwise would put the architect's intervention on a par with suburban home improvements, or the action of squatters in the outskirts of Mexico City.

Where does the distinction lie? In the 1970s, Bernard Rudofsky invoked "architecture without architects" to account for the undeniable beauty and power of vernacular buildings.[16] This stance, conceding that primitive folk could produce something equal to the work of real architects, illustrated how far the profession had removed itself from its roots. The term *informal sector* is often used to indicate vast stretches of fabric produced by the population, itself, without regard to the proposals of government planners and without the help of architects. Yet in the majority of large cities, the informal sector produces more built environment by volume than the formal sector. Paradoxically, architect-designed environment is the exception. However, since those who write, plan and study belong to the formal world, we have adopted an institutional stance in which the normal and age-old way of producing fabric is identified as an anomaly. Over time, the term *informal* has acquired a more neutral meaning. But it emerged with a markedly pejorative connotation when it was no longer possible to deny the existence of that unwelcome reality. Clearly, environmental professionals still seek to distance themselves from the spontaneous age-old process of environmental creation. The term "informal" lends architects and urbanists the illusion of being the legitimate licensed inventors and creators of environmental fabric.

This dilemma is not solved by labeling work by licensed professionals "Architecture" and everything else "vernacular."

Within modern "westernized" cities, where projects are increasingly designed and built by licensed professionals, to declare all buildings "Architecture" would be too painful for many a dedicated designer or critic.[17]

To this day, initiatees into the profession are guided through the streets of Rome or Florence, interrupting their small talk only upon arrival at buildings "of architectural significance." Or they may strike out on their own to see "published" buildings. Renowned streets and squares also make it onto the Grand Tour list. Yet with the exception of well-known cities like Venice or Amsterdam or Paris or Georgian London or Barcelona, the aggregate of buildings and spaces remains an unknown and untaught subject. The urban field is hastily traversed as if it were a meadow or a forest to be crossed to reach the rare bloom that is Architecture.

Once architects got involved with common environment on a massive scale, it was inevitable that "vernacular" architecture would be "discovered" as a well-spring of artistic inspiration. Louis Sullivan taught Frank Lloyd Wright to draw inspiration from nature. But in our increasingly urbanized culture, architects have come to be inspired by buildings. Vernacular building is what brings them closest to nature.

Vernacular building inspired Le Corbusier. The play of immutable volumes and shapes in the strong Mediterranean light led him to discover timeless qualities independent of human action. His inspiration was poetic, not romantic. He did not see complex socially-embedded built fabric, but white-washed volumes that seemed akin to the autonomous forms of factories, grain silos, ocean liners and airplanes conceived by engineers and shaped in steel and concrete.

Aldo van Eyck's inspiration, however, *was* truly romantic. It became an attachment. Like others, he became fascinated with the Dogon and other primitive cultures. He saw spaces of human scale formed by acts of inhabitation; admired the beauty of materials shaped by human hands and the delightful combinations of their colors and textures. In an era dominated by efficiency and standardization, the idea that environment and inhabitation could shape one another in an unending and creative interaction was strangely seductive. Observing the Dogon, van Eyck witnessed the direct interaction between people and their environment. He mourned its loss. This yearning rendered him alien to the Palladian tradition. He could not accept the contemporary practice in which that source had to be rekindled. Instead, he sought the hands-on experience of the vernacular builder.

Where van Eyck discovered form, in Las Vegas Venturi and Scott Brown seemed rather to discover process. The first edition of *Learning from Las Vegas* suggests that "Such a study will help to define a new type of urban form emerging in America and Europe, radically different from what we have known: one that we have been ill equipped to deal with and that, from ignorance, we define today as urban sprawl."[18]

Subsequent editions of the book instead emphasize "a forgotten Symbolism of Architectural Form," thereby resolutely adopting an approach at once more exploitative and poetic, as Le Corbusier had done.[19]

The notion of ordinary environment as the soil from which architecture grows had lain dormant since the time of Palladio. Where Palladio left the field to study ancient architecture as a source for something new, we might study vernacular fields to learn about a process we must become part of. Le Corbusier, Venturi *et al.* and van Eyck effectively rediscovered the living field. But their studies served mainly to underscore the distinction between the field and high architecture. Le Corbusier simply saw in the ordinary a fresh source of inspiring forms and artifacts. These he would appropriate in the way artists had always borrowed from nature. Vernacular architecture interested him only to the extent that it, like other ordinary things, displayed autonomous form. Venturi and Scott-Brown, however, were not preoccupied with form but with the Architect: they sought liberation from modernist stylistic constraints.

Van Eyck, driven by a sense of loss, could not cast off the spell of the Dogon. It rendered him homeless in the profession.

Back in the field again

In contemporary practice, architects are again immersed in the field. We create the flesh and bones of everyday environment. We design places for governing, working, worshipping, learning, healing, commerce, playing and living. What we build becomes part of a living organism larger than anything created by humanity. It is dynamic, vibrant and ever-changing.

Multitude has become the prime environmental issue in modern times. Propelled by demographic developments and the harnessing of energy sources, large numbers translate into entirely new fields of unprecedented extent. They produce suburban prolif-eration on the American continent and largely uncontrollable growth of world cities in Africa, South America, China, Indonesia and elsewhere. In many cases, an over-abundance of small-scale acts produces flat, two-dimensional fields that lack shared spaces or forms to lend identity and orientation. Their landmarks take the form of major road intersections or popular retail outlets.

Large numbers also bring high-rise workplaces, apartment buildings and institutional complexes. These large professional projects with gridded façades may stand together or apart. Either way, they are self-contained, occupying space but seldom forming it. Mid- and low-rise large projects on a massive scale inevitably rubber-stamp doors, windows and entire façades.

In sum, this is the state in which we find our fields. Informal fields continue to produce variety defined and constrained by living

5.1–5.4 The large intervention and the extant field

5.1 Cairo, view from the tower of the Ibn Toulon mosque (9th century AD). The mosque strongly related to its original urban surroundings in terms of craftsmanship. Nonetheless, as a monumental intervention, it overpowered them. Over the centuries, the city's field has grown around it to become a high-density brick-and-concrete field of four- or more story buildings.

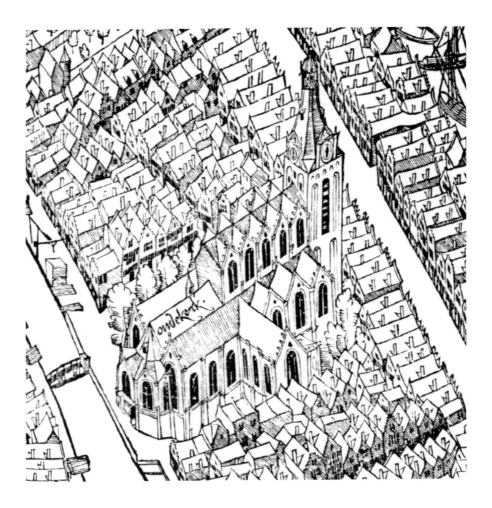

5.2 Amsterdam, the "Old Church," detail of a block print by Cornelis Anthonis, 1544. The church and the surrounding field share craftsmanship, materials and also scale – the bays of the church are about the size of a house lot. Such large and special buildings relate to surrounding buildings as the flower relates to the leaves of its tree. This relationship is commonly seen in historic fields.

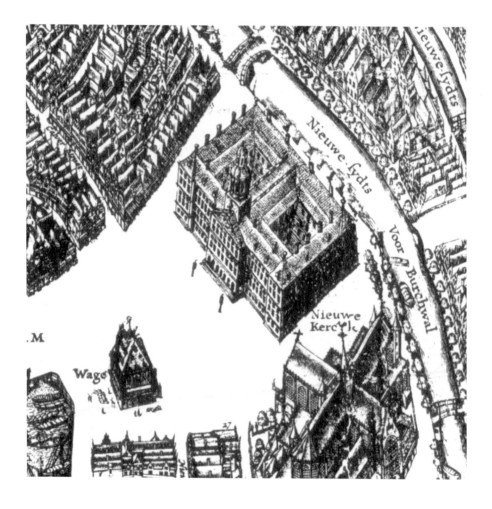

5.3 Amsterdam Town Hall by Jacob van Campen (1648–1665), sited in a much older pre-existing field. After seven years in Italy, van Campen returned to the Netherlands in 1624, where he melded Palladian architecture and neo-classicism with the indigenous brick building culture into Dutch Classicism. Contrasting with the "New Church," this monumental town hall, van Campen's most famous work, represents the prosperous city as the center of a world-wide commercial network. [See also Two: Leaving the Field].

5.4 Paris, Place Vendôme, from the famous 1739 "Turgot" Plan of Paris by Louis Bretez. Jules Hardouin-Mansart designed this monumental intervention on the residential scale within an extant field in 1698 at the request of Louis XIV. His urban design included erection of the façades. Subsequently, wealthy citizens bought lots behind the façades and had their own architects design and build mansions connecting to the façade.

customs and building habits. Yet all too often they develop in a wretched state of improvisation. As for large-scale fields that directly result from professional intervention, their fate appears to be repetition and uniformity. In both cases, the fundamental role of individual inhabitation as a key agent of change, growth and creation has become problematic.

⬤⬤⬤

The major challenge the professional designer encounters in the field is how to meld large-scale intervention with daily living and working. The fundamental difficulties of our return to the field are three-fold.

First of all, there is *change*. The large-scale project must intrinsically sustain partial and uneven change over time if it is to both shelter and sustain small-scale life. But change has always been alien to the Palladian ethos. Our instinct is to defy time and to preserve what we have wrought. The special building – the villa, the palace, the castle, the house of worship – is intended to be immutable in the steadily transforming field: a stone in running waters.

In grafting our own notions of design onto the field, we have understood little of how the field structures itself for inevitable change. The field's dynamics are largely autonomous, and we must learn to respect that autonomy. Architecture as an art form has instead asserted and championed its own autonomy, in ignorance of the broader context in which we build. In mainstream design, growth and change stimulate little creative thinking, or recognition as a source of inspiration leading to a new architecture.

Second, in the traditional field, the small-scale intervention that allows growth, change, and adaptation also implies a *distribution of design responsibility* that involves clients and users as much as environmental professionals or the building trades. The traditional field could incrementally extend itself with continuity in space and time, in ways that dovetailed with traditional modes of intervention. It allowed for different rhythms of change and renewal at different scales of intervention: the town, the building, the room. This no longer worked once modernity had swept away technical, typological, and stylistic habits, while also dramatically increasing the size of interventions. Rootlessness and innovation rendered unified and centralized design control across all scales necessary. Gradually, over the past century, absolute top-down control became the unquestioned pre-condition for good architecture. Yet it has also become untenable by dint of the sheer complexity of the large project: the proliferation of consultant specialists and of subsystems bring into play *de facto* co-designers. Principles of freedom of enterprise and open market demand that such elaborate teams of co-designers be assembled *ad hoc* for each project. As a result, habits of hierarchical control must yield to cooperation. To develop such cooperation and to reconsider the large project as an orchestration of increasingly independent design acts, both in synchronic and sequential order, is the inevitable challenge of our return.

Finally, where design responsibility is distributed, *understandings about form* become important pre-conditions for success. Distribution of intervention produces variety of form. Variety in turn makes us ask what we vary: it reveals structures that we hold in common, but that each of us may interpret differently. If attractive, vital and livable fields inherently display coherence in variety, what brings their cohesiveness about? Our post-modern emphasis on artistic self-expression is far removed from any notion of shared form. We no longer ask what we hold in common. The question is meaningless in the context of sculptural form. Last century's "-isms" denoted preferences that were shared across a globally dispersed professional network. Such commonalities had little bearing on the coherence of fields. What is shared in our fields is bound not to a social group, but to a place. Our return to the field demands a sharing of form, in ways that are new to the globalized profession.

As historic urban fabric reveals, design for the field dynamically balances the three aspects of change, distribution of design responsibility and shared values. Once we are aware of the three leading points of conflict between the field and our Palladian heritage, we observe historic environment anew. Not to copy outmoded forms, but to use past evidence to adopt a successful balance for contemporary environment.

●●●

Sixteenth- and seventeenth-century Dutch cartographers often published bird's eye views of cities. Amsterdam was at that time the world's premiere trade center. It was a favored subject, if only because of its ready market of wealthy citizens who were thrilled to see their town from a vantage point no human being had ever experienced. In those prints, each individual house – seldom seven meters wide – is depicted. Owners could with pride identify their homes within the larger aggregate. Together with the canals, streets, and alleys, the houses form a fine-grained fabric. [Figs 2.1 and 5.2]

The towns are like organisms in which each house is a living cell that can appear, change, grow, die and be replaced in response to the life inhabiting it. Such widespread incremental change is free to occur spontaneously. It requires no immediate response in the larger urban structures. There is a loose fit[1] between social and physical structure: individual houses may contain a shop or workplace in addition to the residence, or else several households. Nonetheless, the relationship is close enough to make the correspondence between life and form mutually responsive. The richness and resilience of that fabric rest on fine-grained individual interventions (houses) framed by large-scale structures (canals).

The cells of urban tissue directly determine the size of the interventions by which renewal takes place. Strings of houses combine to make urban blocks. Blocks strung along canal, river, harbor or bulwark define streets and alleys. In this way, fine-grained fields reveal a rhythmic placement of architectural entities that connect voluntarily, extending from joint to joint. Such joints occur at many different scales, at lot lines, structural bays, party walls, street corners, etc. As the pressure for growth, change or replacement builds, these joints are where acts of transformation encounter the least resistance, where the fabric will most easily tear, or be cut out and replaced. For example, it is easier to demolish a structural bay than to demolish 1½ structural bays. It is easier to rebuild two townhouses than 2½. It is easier to upgrade with furniture that fits within one room than to install furniture that requires demolishing a partition.

The placement of these joints is not arbitrary. Nor is it just physical: their size is determined by a combination of technical constraints, commodity/marketplace forces, territorial boundaries and social preferences. This concurrence of conditions produces what I have previously described as "the structure of the ordinary."[2] Each juncture can act as a boundary between interventions. It defines the grain of the physical fabric as well as the context for design distribution. This universal mechanism allows for vastly different fabrics. Each time, its principles reveal to the patient observer a particular culture of dwelling and building.

In the Qianlong Era map of Beijing, an extended family compound may encompass several courtyards. Each courtyard is in turn formed by pavilions that may shelter a son's family, a workshop or several servant households. [Fig. 3.1] The smallest identifiable cell in the physical fabric is in this case the pavilion; this field is even more fine-grained than the Dutch town. At the other end of the scale was the Venetian Gothic *palazzo* familiar to Andrea Palladio and his clients. Like the Beijing compound, the palazzo might be inhabited by an extended family including servants, yet all were sheltered within a single built volume. [Figs 1.7, 2.3 and 2.4]

These two examples represent the range of sizes within which historic fabrics generally lie. It corresponds to the range that allows inhabitants of the field to renew and transform it cell by cell while the organism persists. Such innate capacity for fine-grained growth and change has for millennia been a well-spring of longevity for fields.

Thematic variation is another byproduct. Where each cell is free to transform, and where the character, extent and rate of transformation are independently determined by individual inhabitants or owners, variety arises naturally throughout the townscape. Occasionally, we find several identical houses in a row as a result of speculative intervention, in which one party builds multiple units, often for subsequent sale. But even in that case, the basic unit of intervention particular to the fabric of the living field is retained. Its size sets the scale of future renewal and change.

●●●

Large-scale projects today frequently occur on an order of magnitude larger than historical interventions. They frequently involve buildings whose volume exceeds, for instance, that of many a classical Greek town.[3] The large-scale project is here to stay and may well become coarser. It all too easily produces uniformity and inflexible repetition that do not respond to life's pulse. How is the architect to reconcile this massive intervention with the fine-grained field? The problem of restoring a more natural environmental relationship between form and inhabitation confronts us in many ways, time and again. From the perspective of the field, this represents the defining challenge of our age: to find a way to restore fine-grained physical character and to create responsive environment within the large project.

At first, reconciling the two may seem impossible. But past and present experience both suggest otherwise. The relation has always been dynamic, but where today the small must find its place in the large, for previous generations the grand gesture of the architect arose from just such fine-grained fabric, lifting the field and its inhabitants to a higher plane. The exceptional act grew from the ordinary as the flower blooms among the leaves of the tree. The same fabric that spawned the humble side streets of medieval Florence produced its domed cathedral and the Foundling Hospital. In the same way, the Rue de Rivoli in Paris, the Georgian crescents of father and son Woods, John Nash's Regents Street and Regents Park and the façades of the Bloomsbury squares succeeded because they grew out of a living fabric already in place. At the same time, they became autonomous urban screens no longer precisely reflecting each house behind.

But these examples remained the exception. Normally in historic fabric, the street wall was an accretion of single interventions over time. These eventually grew to form a continuous virtual public structure, making urban space. Today, this wall can become autonomous as a result of the ongoing changes behind it. In observing this phenomenon, Martin Pawley notes:

> Our growing culture of internal change behind retained façades is . . . beginning to herald the end of the single building as the basic unit of the urban environment, and the beginning of the rule of general purpose serviced floor space.
>
> Take the nineteenth-century façades of the derelict banks in London's Old Broad Street, for example. That part of the City will still be present in a hundred years. But behind these same façades there will be no more wooden floors or high clerk's tables, nor even any party walls. Instead there

will be glass partitions and levels of office floors with a central atrium, cruising over the old divisions between properties.[4]

Were it not mediated by the street wall, the increased scale of intervention would threaten city fabric. When the historical façades of the street wall are preserved, the historical lot lines are still traceable. Behind these, however, wholesale consolidation and intervention take place. Building volumes may extend across historical lot lines, until there are no longer discrete buildings. The phenomenon is not restricted to London, and it amounts to a significant shift in urban structure: such aggregates of façades are becoming stand-alone screens, behind which "buildings" are no longer built. Rather, large three-dimensional structures arise hidden from pedestrian view, waiting to be inhabited in turn. The large volume hidden from public space, may itself be functioning, in turn, as a stable container for fine-grained intervention, one that will transform and renew itself through time.

Such structures no longer correspond to our concept of the discrete and self-contained building. Nor do the street walls that are so painstakingly preserved. As such interventions move toward a new balance, they challenge architecture in many ways. In the process, an entirely new distribution of design responsibilities presents itself.

The autonomous façade may also manifest itself in reverse fashion. Whether its form is that of a tower block or of a mega-block, the curtain wall façade of the large contemporary building, less durable than the steel or concrete frame it clads, may be exchangeable. This skin may well be shed several times over the life-time of the building, its design radically altered.[5] As our stock of modernist buildings ages, redesign of the façade during renovation is becoming commonplace. Such architectural design is leading to another new approach to the distribution of design tasks. Just as there are currently technical curtain wall specialists, commissions for façade design of new buildings may eventually fall to someone other than the building architect.

The preserved small-scale historic façade and the shorter-lived skin of the large building both have a rationale in contemporary culture. To recognize this is to perceive that we are only one step removed from independently designing autonomous street walls, rather than designing them as part of the construction behind them. There is historic precedent for this, as well. In late seventeenth-century Paris, Jules Hardouin-Mansart, architect to the king, designed the façades of the Place Louis-le-Grand. The resulting wall encloses what is now known as the Place Vendôme. It was built by Mansart in a single intervention. What happened behind the façade was left entirely to the wealthy citizens who, one by one, purchased and built on the empty lots beyond. [Fig. 5.4] As Michael Dennis observes, "the combination of regular stability in the public realm and irregular variety in the private realm represents an urban concept of great potential."[6] Mansart's design was executed for the same reason that historic façades in contemporary cities are now preserved throughout the world.

Similarly, in the renovation of Phillip III's Plaza Mayor in Madrid, the front six or eight feet of the extant houses were summarily excised and rebuilt as a unified street wall with loggias. Again in Paris, in the case of the Place Royale, lot owners were contractually obligated to build independent buildings with a predetermined façade design that formed part of a uniform wall around the public space.[7]

In each case, to respond to extant living fabric, design responsibility in large-scale intervention was divided in a new way. This increased the scope of intervention on the urban scale while preserving private intervention on a smaller scale. The result was a new interplay between two kinds of designers, the architect and the

5.5 Paris, Place Vendôme. [See also Fig. 5.4]

urban designer. Such innovative and unfamiliar design distribution offered great freedom to design and build private space, while ensuring the harmonious character of the public realm. It cut across conceptual, territorial and professional boundaries, and also clean through the habitual understanding of the "building" as singular product arising out of a self-contained act.

Today, a similar shift toward distributed design intervention is found in the commercial office building. There, the shift in design approach was not in response to urban-scale coherence. Rather, it responded directly to the need for fine-grained inhabitation to find its place within the large project. It brings changes that will eventually overtake all disciplines involved. It emerged slowly, over time, in response to market demand and tenant desire to rejoin the environmental game and to control and determine the character of one's own space as in times past. Out of this process, this unprecedented scale and condition, an entirely new form of

5.6 Paris, Place des Vosges (formerly Place Royale), 1739. Detail of the "Turgot" Plan of Paris by Louis Bretez. Private citizens built adjoining houses that incorporated uniform pre-determined façades.

5.7 Paris, Place des Vosges. View of the façades.

tenancy and of design – variously known as *infill architecture*, *tenant improvements* or *fit-out* – has emerged.

High-rise office and commercial structures are popularly conceptualized as "buildings" akin to gigantic houses. With respect to their scale, design processes, utilities routing and use, however, they are rather chunks of three-dimensional urban fabric. For all practical purposes, they function like gated neighborhoods. [Fig. 6.2] With the increasing presence of the car in the urban fabric, the pedestrian realm is moving inside. Interior space is replacing or extending in character and uses the squares and streets that have grown so familiar from medieval times on. Far from becoming endangered, pedestrian environment is adapting to changed conditions. What are we to make of such interior public space? How can it bloom, come into its own architecturally? The first design explorations of such space have been uncertain, tentative, at times superficial. The large building's corridors and hallways –

particularly above the entry and retail levels – still repeat patterns from the bygone days of the villa and the townhouse or, worse yet, the nineteenth-century institutional building. Finding the true expression of public interior space presents an unprecedented architectural challenge. Thus far, although design distribution is a well-established fact in the contemporary office building, it has not inspired a new architecture.

Within suburban fields, the contemporary shopping mall reveals a distribution of design responsibility similar to that of the office building. As retail space inhabits the larger structure, the interior façades of leased mall space have become to varying degrees autonomous. We are witnessing the embryonic emergence of a peculiar fabric whose full architectural potential is clearly not yet understood. Despite the introduction of atrium space, escalators and food courts, this interplay of architectural interventions on multiple levels has yet to find a convincing balance of expression between retail occupancy and public spaces. [Fig. 6.3]

Such dialogue between old and new ways and the systems that embody them dominates urban renewal and growth. As the scale of contemporary intervention increases, the field's need to render the size of interventions harmonious with both social structure and physical form teaches us new ways of working with new emerging systems. It is the well-spring of innovation.

●●●

Throughout history, architecture and building had always been systematic, in the sense that ways of building rested on shared elements brought together in fixed and familiar ways. Even two generations ago, architects still learned and practiced vernacular conventions of detailing doors and windows, roofs and frames. Change flowed back and forth between the field and the profession: standards in the field evolved as much from design as from hands-on construction. In detailing materials, the architect's touch expressed itself as a variation on conventional ways of building. It seldom attempted to circumvent or supplant them, or the way of life they embodied.

The schism between architectural design and conventional building systems is a rather recent development. It was unknown in the Renaissance, or in the centuries following. Only during the modern era did conventional context begin to evaporate. Jean Prouvé, Konrad Wachsmann and Walter Gropius beheld the future: they understood that it belonged to industrial production. Its systems would have a profound impact on the look and feel of environment. For that reason, they cast architectural design in a dual role: followed by numerous others, Gropius *et al.* wanted to invent the system as well as the building made from it. They dreamed that architects would marry architecture and industrial systems, that industry and building culture would follow their lead.[8]

Systems are created by complex forces. The ones that persist – whether technical or aesthetic – reflect the needs and values of an entire society. Looking backward, it is also clear that technical innovation has been driven by sectors other than architecture. Value added to projects by offsite manufactured systems – from building structure to environmental systems to kitchens and baths – has been steadily increasing for over a century. Value added on-site by conventional general contractors and sub-contractors has been decreasing.[9] As this trend continues, architecture increasingly becomes the art of deploying available systems in response to client needs and site constraints. This represents an entirely new kind of design distribution. The industrial designer who shapes a new material or a system such as a glass curtain wall may have a vastly larger impact on environmental character and quality than any architect who uses that system. Here too, the field defies familiar notions about the boundaries of architecture.

Architects, like ancient master builders and other guild members, identify themselves by association with certain systems, in which they develop expertise. In some cases – cut and stacked stone for cathedral builders, prairie-style masonry and carpentry for Frank Lloyd Wright, glazed curtain wall and steel frame for SOM during the heyday of the modernist era, wide or contorted bands of metal clad structure for Frank Gehry, etc. – preferred systems have become "signature" elements. This may prove to be vestigial, a left-over from historic times when architects lived their entire lifetime within a stable system. In a pluralistic world where global reference is commonplace, systemic self-identification may become a liability for the general practitioner. Systems selection may increasingly become a matter that is locally determined. It may be based on ability to lend identity to a particular place while architectural mastery is expected to enhance, by elaboration and interpretation, what is already thematic.

The designer *of* the system provides a specific product. Its interface with other products is well defined and its performance is carefully specified, but the system is otherwise open to combining and recombining. The designer working *with* a system pushes it to maximize unique application. The mindset needed for each of these two design tasks is different: the system is something to be shared among a variety of designers, its application is a unique and local act.

The interdependence between the two is the hallmark of contemporary environment, and has grown more complex over time. Yet the two ways of design thinking – design of the shared and design of the singular – are not limited to systematization. More generally, their dialectic is characteristic of all thematic design. It is found as well in the relation between type and variant, or between a pattern and a specific instance of the pattern. Often the two modes of design thinking are close and their interaction can be direct, but they naturally lend themselves to distributed design tasks. Architectural quality depends on both in equal measure.

However, many systems in a building are not within the design scope of the architect. Within the building as a composition of systems, the architect is neither the designer *of* all systems, nor does he or she design *with* all systems. Much design is now conventionally performed by engineers and other specialized consultants. Throughout all phases of design, they contribute as designers in their own right. Thus, the increased proliferation of sub-systems has led to an increased distribution of responsibility in the actual design of the architecture. The architect orchestrates and coordinates. Paradoxically, while consultant design may not appear prominently in the completed project, it frequently establishes dimensions, spans, story heights, and other fundamental aspects of architectural character. Coordination is the singular greatest challenge of many projects.

As larger architecture is parsed into smaller responsibilities, and as the design of base building types and infill becomes increasingly specialized, diverse teams of architects must collaborate and coordinate as well. Such teaming within the discipline has become a norm in institutional practice. Many architects in practice never actually design an entire building by themselves. Rather, their careers are shaped by the various design tasks the large intervention entails.

The concept of the unitary building, when applied to a massive intervention, is at once less clear-cut and less helpful than we are accustomed to thinking. Increasingly the structure of the field leads the profession to conceive of new ways of intervening and collaborating. Ultimately, the field requires highly complex interaction between designers, each in control of his or her domain, yet working in cooperation.

And that is the dilemma. From a traditional perspective, within a profession whose self-image is built upon the Renaissance ideology of full control of the villa-sized project, we devalue the "partial design" inherent in contemporary intervention. But as they play out across the urban space of the field, it is precisely such well-defined, intricately coordinated, interdependent but autonomous design moves, within the bounds and levels defined by the field's intrinsic structure, that sustain the field and build continuity. The façade, the base building, the actual inhabitation – each has the potential to contribute directly to the field's fabric. Each contribution entails a variety of subsystems representing different expertise. Individual interventions, each less than an entire building, add to a whole much larger than the building.

For some, the emergence of this reality is anathema; it represents a further dilution of the architect's role. It defies habitual concepts. Above all, it questions the iconic self-contained building as the measure of all architecture. The source of this unfamiliar environmental game is far-removed from manufacturing and technology. Its well-spring lies in our intuitive ability to seek within thematic coherence the basis for individual identity. In the historic field, the two went hand in hand. It is only in recent times that we have abandoned thematic variation to exclusively pursue unique identity. In our return to the field, themes that for millennia have been the binding force of fields and the cultures they envelope rise up to meet us, but in entirely new ways.

Historic images of Amsterdam are again instructive. In the eighteenth century, Caspar Philips Jacobsz. depicted entire street walls, portraying every individual façade lining the three major canals. His prints reveal a strongly thematic architecture, maintained and subtly transformed over generations. We see in those prints a wonderful harmony of individual expression. Some façades stay close to one another in intent and execution – their

5.8 Amsterdam, façades along the Herengracht, ca. 1767. From a book of measured drawings by Caspar Philips.

fenestration, brick detailing, entries, story heights and roofscapes are quite similar. Others stray a bit. Within their general kinship, clear types can be distinguished.

In every case, each canal house plays off of the surrounding themes and, by elaboration and particular interpretation, adds to them. The accumulation of so many of these interventions balances the monumental horizontal structure of the canals. Each house is a discrete, well-bounded presence. Yet stoops strung along the street wall lend an urban continuity on the pedestrian scale. Gables combine into a block-long undulating profile. Such common themes run through the aggregate of these street walls, defining and identifying them like the veins of a polished slab of marble.

Such thematic unity is the way of fields. Each field we enter, new or old, persists in that way. Each designer's contributions to it vary. Some set themes, some elaborate them, some shift themes. Yet others, in the design of a larger structure, frame subsequent thematic play by designers within the spaces it defines.

Design, whether of a city center or a modest room addition, always adds to a larger whole, and always makes spaces for subsequent intervention. From the perspective of the field, all intervention is partial. Identity of form has many faces and design has many voices: urban space, façade, base building for residential or commercial inhabitation, interior public space, tenant fit-out, theatrical set-piece within an existing volume. Each intervention is a sufficient and legitimate contribution to the field; a statement unto itself, yet impossible without its context. We inhabit fields that record the passing of many hands. They are composed of countless interventions, all of which are dignified for the profession.

In both historic and contemporary vernacular environment, thematic restatement of the typology is not the result of deliberate design: it is rooted in age-old processes of human interaction. This heritage helps to explain the field and its ongoing interventions. Vernacular and professional themes coexist in a continuum from the predominantly implicit to the more explicit. There is no clear-cut dividing line between the two. But what is neither said nor noted is the most stable of all. Thematic rules reside in the forms themselves as they evolve. We may live with them for years, only to become aware of them when they are violated. For instance, in American suburbia, fences set up along streets with formerly open lawns generate protest: we become aware of the qualities of fence-less environment which had been taken for granted.

The thematic is local. When entering an unfamiliar culture, its fields may be incomprehensible. In the course of time, we discover underlying kinship: there are types, patterns and styles, revealing a "method in the madness".[10] Eventually, we no longer take note. With familiarity, the thematic is taken for granted, it becomes self-evident, implicitly understood and entirely unremarkable.

With each variation we make, we confirm the broader theme. Our variant not only conforms; it also identifies our intervention, because no other is precisely the same. We may invent a certain twist, challenge the rules. As others pick up on the innovation, the theme will eventually evolve to encompass it. Or else it will dwell in isolation, remaining an oddity. Thus, in a healthy formal interplay, the actual rules remain largely implicit. Like musicians, we are very good at improvising, picking up a theme and running with it: it is best when we play by ear. Thematic sensitivity is innate, and also what gives rise to styles and fashions. Neighbors tend to conform to local patterns and customs, and to "keep up with the Joneses." But at the same time they want to show their own identity.

The causes of thematic coherence are many. They include the practical – technology, ways of working, ways of use – as much as cosmology and culture. This heritage helps to explain the contemporary field and its ongoing interventions. Although the scale of interventions has increased and the combinations and interactions have grown more complex in contemporary environment, the well-springs of coherence still flow. Yet from the point of view of a profession whose identity and body of knowledge have become increasingly self-referential, our return to the field of the everyday and the ordinary brings us into uncharted territory.

In contrast to the past, the contemporary field recognizes no divide between vernacular and Architecture. In the context of an evolving profession that designs the humble and the monumental, the sacred and the profane, the distinction is meaningless. The implications of that fact are uncertain for both the profession and the field. This is where our theorizing on architecture needs to focus. At the very least, we may thereby escape the isolation from the common which is Alberti's legacy, while celebrating the clarity of our Palladian heritage of well-crafted design.

Our return to the field thus sets into play a new game, at once more subtle and more complex. To be successful we need not shed our recent heritage as much as we need to temper it with a new level of sophistication that demands new skills and knowledge.

Ways of working   SIX

Fields changed profoundly in the centuries following Palladio.
That much is clear to lay person and professional alike. The scale
and complexity of intervention increased. New building materials,
systems, building types and utilities took root. Global markets,
information networks and services appeared. Such new circumstances demand new expertise. Yet while conditions have increasingly led to fundamental changes in architectural practice, the
architect's role was last fundamentally re-examined when Alberti
proclaimed that henceforth the architect would be free from the
constraints of local habit and convention.

Alberti understood that new circumstances demand new ways
of working. He also contemplated the expertise associated with that
new role. Abandoning vernacular routine and rules of thumb,
Alberti tried to pin down how designers conceive and organize
form in three-dimensional space, and suggested the means of *linea-*
menta. The ability to freely invent form in space has preoccupied
architects ever since. Rooted in the Renaissance, it has remained the
profession's guiding star for almost five centuries.

In modern times, architecture has witnessed increased material
and spatial complexity in the field, new patterns of control, new
types of clients, new client and building types, systems and
processes, new modes of transportation, new networks and vastly
increased size and numbers. Architects have accepted international
codes, computers, computer-based modeling and engineering and

~ 130 ~

6.1–6.4 The vertical field

6.1 View of Tokyo from the Shiodome Building, 2003. Typical example of a contemporary medium-scale metro-politan field. The fabric still respects the urban spatial grid. However, the size of the buildings makes them function as small independent neighborhoods served by vertical dead-end streets.

6.2 Plaza view of Ludwig Mies van der Rohe's high-rise Chicago Federal Center (1959-74), with Alexander Calder's "Flamingo" in the foreground. In most contemporary office buildings, the uniform and repetitive outer skin belies the fact that the interior can be adapted in response to tenant preferences. Most office buildings offer raw floor space as territory for lease. The lessee privately engages designers and contractors to fit it out. In that sense, office building environment serves as a fine-grained vertical neighborhood capable of partial change over time.

6.3 Cambridge, Massachusetts, Lechmere shopping mall. The contemporary shopping mall also functions as a fine-grained three-dimensional field. Public space structures the fabric while individual shops design their own territories.

6.4 Hong Kong residential district. Hong Kong is the ultimate extremely high density vertical field. 40-story residential buildings have become a norm. Unfortunately, the apartment interiors have become increasingly inflexible over time. Hong Kong is now a coarse-grained field in which renewal or change must occur throughout an entire building at one time. Such buildings will likely prove unable to accommodate inhabitants' future demands.

electronic production and information exchange including CAD, the Internet, email, electronic file exchange, word processing and automated business processes. Sweeping changes in communication, interaction, coordination, production and construction have fundamentally changed the way architects work, collaborate, coordinate and present.

Most importantly, clients have become more and more institutionalized and society has established increasingly complex rules of performance and procedure. The profession has produced enormous hands-on innovation in response to the field. Nonetheless, none of this has led the profession to fundamentally re-examine how we actually practice design. On the contrary, the profession has pragmatically adjusted its ways *ad hoc* while clinging steadfastly to an outdated and frequently contradictory ideology. Questions regarding methodology have seldom entered the mainstream of architectural theory and education.

An ideology of invention and artistic self-expression has scant use for methodology. And with good reason: beyond a certain point, the creative process remains mysterious in every discipline. Ways of working may be based on creativity but need not explain it. Methodology comes to the fore only when discrete design tasks are interrelated. Methods are of interest when we see our work as contingent upon interventions by other designers and other parties making design decisions. This contingency is precisely what Alberti sought to escape. It confronts us again on our return to the field.

●●●

Change, distribution of design responsibility and sharing of form conventions – the three major points of conflict between our ideology and the demands of the field – *all* involve relations among designers. The moment we perceive these relations not only as inevitable, but also as important and desirable, we will seek out ways of facilitating and structuring work accordingly. Where urban design and architecture intersect, things such as set-back rules provide a way. Similarly, the very use of any dimensional system is a fundamental tool to avoid confusion where a task is handed down, or relegated to a lower level. Methodology is neither a denial of the central role of creative power, nor a diversion from it. It sees design as fundamentally more than inventing form. Its task is to make sure that creative energy remains meaningful and effective in even the most complex situations.

●●●

In the design studio around which our educational system revolves, inventing form is synonymous with design. It is the focus of our professional training. Semester after semester, students individually design free-standing schematic buildings the size of Palladio's Villa Rotonda or Church of the Redentore. They learn to control form at a building size that is ideal for signature design, for architectural monologue and singular design control. Not surprisingly, architects subsequently do their best work when designing isolated free-standing formal objects at a mid-size project range. It is what we value and relate to above all else.

The history of architecture is generally portrayed in this light. It presents a portfolio of brilliant designers who invented just such architectural gems and marvels through each passing age, individuals who offered the world previously unknown experiences and forms of beauty.

Yet in the natural history of fields, all design is partial: form – whether a modest house addition or the Guggenheim Museum in Bilbao – always contributes to a larger whole. In that broader context, the inspiring architectural record of signature design seems less considered and less significant. How could it be otherwise? Our inherited Palladian model could not have prepared us for the game rules imposed by the field. Such field-generated aspects of the work-life of architects – collaborating, sustaining local typologies, setting up thematic principles, extending coherence and spatial continuity – are not supported by the profession's venerable design traditions. Torn between the ideology of the past and the realities of the field, architects publish and promote uncompromisingly Palladian successes while maintaining silence about so much work that is essentially integrative.

Founded upon work in isolation, self-expression and uncon-strained creative freedom, the ethos of the design *atelier* creates scant need for method. It is therefore not surprising that Alberti's theory of *lineamenta*, which approached a methodological theory, was simply never developed.

Nonetheless, the architectural profession could not have sur-vived had ways of working not evolved. In daily practice, architects continually cope with the field's demands for coordination, design distribution and collaboration, albeit with varying degrees of willingness, interest, understanding and success. Yet in all cases they do so without benefit of knowledge grounded in mainstream disciplinary theory or education.

Wherever designers relate, method, usually unnamed and unrecorded, emerges. Inexorably, the profession's return to the field forces architects to distribute design responsibilities. It demands routines that make relations among designers work smoothly and effectively. Where design interventions by different parties dovetail, the need to preserve the freedom of individuals to control design becomes urgent. This calls for well-defined boundaries between domains of responsibility and for conventions and tools that make the interface succeed. From a Palladian perspective, any need to accept interactive design on multiple levels spells further dilution of the architect's domain. But understood in the context of the living field, it presents an entirely new game with its own space for invention and creativity, inspiring forms and fine-grained processes that would otherwise remain impossible.

●●●

Relationships between designers operating in the field come in recognizable categories. A profession dedicated to the field needs to study them. Knowledge of their dynamics is a prerequisite of our successful return to the field.

Design relations are either *horizontal* or *vertical*.[1] *Horizontal distribution* of design comprises the relations we engage in as equals who are free to share values, preferences and common space within the larger context of the field. This occurs when architects design harmonious buildings in a shared location. It is "horizontal" in the sense that, while neither building nor designer necessarily dominates the other, they do at the same time relate in space through a shared context. When buildings along a road, surrounding a square or within a city block are individually renovated or replaced, they inevitably relate as parts within a larger whole. This kind of participation straddles the boundary of the implicit and the explicit. It is thematic and non-hierarchical.

In *vertical distribution*, on the other hand, the relations between designers are hierarchical. Design intervention by a "higher level" party frames subsequent interventions by designers on a "lower level." Differently stated, the higher-level designer provides a "site" for lower-level designers to build within. In this way, urban form frames building form and building form frames interior design. These environmental hierarchies of form directly structure relationships between designers: decisions made by the urban designer subsequently constrain the architect; and decisions made by the architect subsequently constrain the interior designer. This hierarchy, in which intervention and physical form coincide, is intuitively familiar; it is a fundamental structuring principle of environmental order.

In all forms, both natural and man-made, complexity spawns hierarchy. As the number of parts to be controlled multiplies, a higher level is established to structure their presence and interaction. The leaves of the tree are held aloft by twigs, the twigs by branches, the branches by the trunk. The computer has a motherboard. The car's many parts used to be held together by the chassis, now they are framed by the body shell. In environmental form, frameworks in steel, concrete, masonry or wood hold varied and overlapping systems in place. In all cases, the framework remains constant while the dependent systems change. Such higher-level structures situate lower-level intervention, but also create freedom for lower-level change.

However, during its infrequent transformations, higher-level form will disturb what it encompasses. The cutting of a highway through extant fabric disturbs the urban grid. When a road is realigned, buildings that line the curb must adjust or be demolished; when the base building is taken down, so are the tenant spaces within; when interior partitions are shifted, the furniture they enclose must move. In all cases, the same asymmetrical interaction applies: environmental change reverberates downward, but not upward. Distributed design control directly reflects this intrinsic physical order.

In the social order of environment, freedom to act demands stratification of responsibilities. Failure to delegate action produces both the dictator and the mob. In physical organization as well, lack of delegation easily results in oppressive and unnatural repetition, as witnessed in the mass housing that arose in the aftermath of

World War II. Or, where there are endless individual interventions and no larger structure, the result can be mindless sprawl.

By contrast, where design is distributed among multiple levels, the thematic variation on which living fields depend appears spontaneously. Planners, urban designers, architects, fit-out designers, interior designers and furniture designers all have a place working within this hierarchical order. On each level of intervention, higher-level form structures space, developing themes and capacities for lower-level follow-up. From the traditional perspective of making stand-alone design statements, architects perceive the constraints of higher-level form as inevitable. The profession has therefore grown to begrudgingly accept such constraints as a creative challenge. Architects are far less willing to accept that ceding downward control – making space to enable subsequent lower-level design by others – is a creative act of design.

Environmental hierarchy may also differ between cultures. Traditional Japanese architecture harbored no furniture, nor is it found in the vernacular houses of the Trulli in southern Italy. Yet in any given order, boundaries between existing levels of intervention need not be rigidly fixed: they may be negotiable. In Mansart's façades in the Place Vendôme, design that normally occurred on the building level incidentally became part of the larger urban design. [Figs 5.4 and 5.5] Today as well, façades may operate in either domain. The curtain wall that normally expresses the large steel-framed building may – following renovation if not by initial design – become an urban-scale intervention. As such, it can shape urban space or urban building profiles rather than express project interiors. It can respond to the spaces it borders, rather than merely wrapping the building volume.

Domains of intervention can accordingly shift as technical systems, social organization or values change. In multi-tenant office building cores, gang toilets form part of higher-level base building design, whereas in luxury apartments, bathrooms form part of the lower-level fit-out. Heat and hot water for multiple tenants in a variety of building types used to be provided by a common furnace or boiler. Today, environmental controls, water heaters and associated energy costs are increasingly distributed, individually controlled by each tenant.

A margin for negotiation between levels thus helps to ensure the long-term stability of the field. But the environmental hierarchy itself may eventually shift under pressure. Although largely set by scale, gravity and enclosure, it can be profoundly affected by shifts in cultural preferences and technical developments. The emergence of a furniture level into Japan's environmental structure happened at a time when built environment was rapidly transforming throughout the world. New modes of transportation were introduced. Utility systems proliferated. There arose functional building types never before seen.

As a result, traditional hierarchical order broke down. Environment grew coarser and environmental understandings became over-simplified. Building types that for centuries had joined together to form continuous urban fabric were abandoned. With them, the level of urban structure that they had responded to disappeared. As public space lost its structuring power, cities and towns came to be shaped by free-standing building volumes. At the same time, changes in technology and logistics, coupled with shifts in social control and the distribution of capital, brought forth larger and larger interventions.

Architects responded to the challenge posed by this violent transformation of environmental order with a habitual Palladian reflex. The solution seemed obvious: more design and more centrally controlled design would produce better environment. Ludwig Mies van der Rohe, Frank Lloyd Wright and Le Corbusier taught us to single-handedly control environment, designing from the building shell down to the light fixtures, the dinner table and the pattern of the place setting. To a generation that experienced the upheavals of modernism, the past was inevitably found wanting. Lacking an understanding of the loss of environmental order, the logic of such projects was compelling. They were viewed as a testimony to the fact that invention and talent would secure a good and elegant future.

This denial of environmental hierarchy formed part of a general preference for top-down control among all professionals involved in environmental intervention. For a brief period of time, spanning perhaps a professional generation or two, the conjunction of full vertical design control and vastly expanding project size seemed to promise a new and better world. Virtue and power seemed to go hand in hand. The assumption of absolute vertical design control produced Le Corbusier's *Plan Voisin*, Tony Garnier's *Cité Industrielle* and the iconic residences that architects worldwide celebrate as the jewels of modernism.

Vertical design control is still regarded among architects as the ideal condition for producing good form. As a result, the potential for a radically new architecture, one designed by many masters operating at many levels, remains virtually unexplored. Yet at the same time, the field is reasserting its fine-grained structure in new ways. In the midst of these ongoing changes, all actors have become increasingly enmeshed in complex webs of interaction and coordination.

●●●

Delegation of control spawns multiple actors on a lower level. It sets the stage for horizontal relations among designers. Through the ages, horizontal relations have produced coherence-in-variety. While variety is the inevitable and happy result of distributed design control, the sources of coherence are many. It is natural for actors on a given level to share common influences – not only physical context and climatic conditions, but also ways of working, ways of building, use of commonly available systems and materials, and conventional detailing.

Nonetheless, the profound coherence of fields springs from deeper sources. Call it *style* or *custom*, *tradition* or *habit* or *building culture*: social preference has always been a defining factor. There is no reason to believe that factor has diminished in contemporary society. On the contrary, as information becomes global and material goods are more and more easily distributed, social preference in its many manifestations may become more dynamic and versatile. Nonetheless, it remains all-important to the unity of inhabitation and form.

For the designer in the field, the implications of this are profound. Practitioners were historically embedded in the vernacular. The themes of the field were fixed constraints. Socio-cultural preferences could not be separated from available techniques, climate and habits of building to which the designer was beholden. To today's global practitioner, these aspects are variables that change from field to field. No longer predetermined, they become active thematic opportunities.

Before the profession abandoned the field in the Renaissance era, the field had long represented a severe constraint. Now, upon our return, it embodies a design challenge. Each field demands that we apply new knowledge and new skills in which type, pattern and system are sophisticated tools. Coherence-in-variety no longer results from inevitable traditions and habits. It has become the product of architectural expertise in support of social preference.

◐◐◐

Designers will always be involved in horizontal and vertical relations with other designers. To cultivate fields, we must understand the broad spectrum of ways of interacting. This knowledge spawns methods that help us to navigate relations in the field as positive and inspiring conditions for creative design. It will determine our success in returning to the field.

Such design methods have little to do with procedures. In design, as in all creative action, predetermined recipes are of little or no use. Design methodology's major objective is to make operational the distribution of design responsibilities. Certain crucial questions must be answered time and again: To what extent is a given design task autonomous? At what point must it interface with others? The more clearly interface conditions, boundaries and limits of responsibility are defined, the more freedom each designer enjoys within his or her own domain. Consequently, the less time needs to be spent on negotiation, compromise, building consensus and redesigning. Interface conditions, boundaries and limits of responsibility are what method is about.

Thus, the first task of methodology is to help us settle who controls what within the field. Boundary conditions, once established, raise the issue of shared values. In horizontal coordination, decisions about thematic development are in order. Types and patterns must be agreed upon. For instance, what characteristics should houses along a street or buildings in a campus have in common? Spatial organization? Materiality? Color? Key dimensions? Patterns of entry and enclosure?

While defining horizontal relations, thematic rules also frame vertical relations. Urban design specifications for a given streetscape may prescribe set-backs, rights of way, impervious coverage or height restrictions. Or they may prescribe certain materials or colors. The design of a base building may anticipate a certain type of lower-level fit-out tenancy in its bay sizes, interstitial spaces, utilities and public space provisions. Thus thematic principles serve horizontal and vertical decisions simultaneously.

The distribution of design tasks is also directly connected to the complex distribution of responsibilities among the trades who sequentially assemble and install components and sub-systems during construction. The higher-level superstructure must accommodate a range of assemblies for partitioning, environmental conditioning and transporting wastes, power, gas, water and data. The internal hierarchy of each supply sub-system piped throughout the building may in turn require independent coordination at each of the various levels of the building.

Even when the scope of design and installation is assigned to consultants, the design of architectural space and structure nevertheless includes locating chases, plenums and interstitial spaces with adequate capacity to install, maintain and eventually replace sub-systems. Based largely on sequencing of trades, architects also can and do stipulate that primary responsibility for coordination falls to one contractor or another, establishing a hierarchical pecking order where multiple systems meet. Such methods of temporal and spatial coordination amount to traffic management in an attempt to avoid systems collisions in unforeseen places. While the issue is highly technical, it presents profound conceptual implications for the design of buildings.

In response to the demands of the field, a three-step ordering principle has begun to emerge: First, domains of design control are identified. Next, distribution of design control asks what is to be shared – be it actual physical interfaces and boundaries, common space or principles of form. Finally, there are necessary agreements about such sharing: to express values, settle boundaries of control, choose thematic aspects, etc. Here methodology's most tangible task is apparent: it provides tools for coordination and agreement. Set-back rules, for instance, are methodological tools for specific positioning of buildings. Grids form the basis for a variety of rules and agreements about the placement of objects in space. Patterns are conceptual tools employed to come to agreement about the use of objects and their relations in space. Types and systems likewise are tools of agreement to do certain things in a similar way while leaving room for variation. Three-dimensional modeling in CAD programs is, among many other things, a tool to convey the look and feel of a proposed scheme, thereby establishing a basis for understanding among parties.

The toolbox does not tell the carpenter what to make, nor in what sequence to apply the tools. But it does define the range of his art: a well-appointed toolbox forms the basis for a successful product. It enlarges the domain of possible products and increases the likelihood of success, whether the goal is artistic, personal, professional or oriented toward business processes. In the same way, methodology does not provide a recipe or tell designers what to do first or last. Methods, including the tools incorporating them, want to be as value-free as possible. Rules of conduct such as set-backs may establish quantified values. But set-back rules more generally establish a relation between urban designer and architect, allowing them to agree on the actual distance to be observed. Tools, understood in this way, help us to specify and uphold values. Nonetheless, they themselves are value-neutral. Methodology, as a subject for research and development, is thus one step removed from making value judgments. Within a discipline that lives by value judgment, this may be another reason why methods are rarely actively pursued.

Methods are of compelling interest to designers only in cases where design cannot succeed without them. Such design settings are where they must be acquired. Designing two custom apartments or free-standing dwellings or commercial architectural interiors simultaneously poses no great challenge. A student may even manage to successfully design ten. But absent a methodological approach, the problem of simultaneously designing a hundred or a thousand different interior layouts – particularly for real and unique clients – becomes insurmountable. At that point, the concepts of type, pattern, and system are no longer abstractions: they become practical tools that provide an alternative to the uniform repetition endemic to the large project. As instruments for thematic design, these concepts help to distinguish constant features from those that may vary. They allow many sets of hands to proceed independently in coordinated variation. Adopting adequately described typological elements while defining their relations and hierarchical importance is a methodological issue. Subsequent value judgments – how to handle a particular agreed-upon type, where to draw the line between theme and variation – are questions of judgment, not method.

Again, such methods have appeal only when architects are no longer convinced that rotating a handful of cookie cutter units is an adequate response to the needs of diverse households and individuals. The tools, in turn, allow us to confidently design complex and varied artifacts of a magnitude we could otherwise not attempt. Once we understand this, understand the limits of what any one designer can efficiently do, and also observe how ordinary environment structures coherent variety, we see merit in the distribution of design responsibility.

Concepts such as type and level, pattern and system lie at the core of architectural cooperation. These conceptual tools have long been used intuitively. Agreement arises only when there is a desire to work together. What can be made explicit is already rooted in the vast domain of intuition and affinity out of which we instinctively interconnect. The concept of type, for instance, is important precisely because it straddles the implicit and the explicit. There is no clear dividing line between the two. As a tool, it cannot derive solely from invention or research. Like the word that denotes it, it is a collective creation that lives within a social body, a product of our need for human interaction. Such concepts were already deeply embedded within the culture of building long before the architect's emancipation from the field. But our re-entry makes them new and more pertinent.

●●●

Ultimately, design decisions boil down to selecting forms, elements and systems and determining where, precisely, they will be placed. This information must be efficiently and unambiguously – which is to say, methodically – conveyed to other parties, who in turn add their own design or execute the design. Proper selection of elements has spawned tools of specification and naming that connect to much larger issues of product classification. Placing objects in space relative to one another, has, among other tools, spawned grids to distribute a building's elements in space. Normally used to aid in the orderly disposition of columns or load-bearing walls, the use of formal grids can be traced back beyond the Renaissance. On occasion, their use has been inspired and original, as in the way Frank Lloyd Wright reinvented them to serve hexagonal and triangular spatial organizations.

The utility of such grids in helping to communicate the placement of architectural elements is self-evident. To that end, when distribution of design involves physical parts controlled by multiple parties operating on different levels, grids should support a positioning tool like the universal GPS system. Unfortunately, grids have acquired a bad name in architecture because they, like industrial production, were used extensively in an era of deadening repetition and uniformity. But there are rigid and loose grid conventions, and the grid as a conventional positioning tool need not predetermine form any more than global coordinates predetermine sea routes. The grid simply allows us to locate building parts. As traffic lanes are designated to avoid collisions in well-traveled seas or skies, placement rules in architectural grids allow parts controlled by different designers to be placed independently within tight and highly coordinated spaces.

In architecture, the choice of a grid remains a design decision like the choice of a harmonic scale in musical composition. Once chosen, it sets the tone while remaining open to various positioning rules. The conflation of repetitive form in architecture and rules for positioning objects in space has left underdeveloped our ability to locate all parts appropriately in design and construction. Our methods for coordinating work and delimiting boundaries among levels, systems, designers and contractors remain primitive. They are to a large extent conventional, *ad hoc* and implicit. As a result, major conflicts between structure, ductwork, piping, shafts and wall and floor openings – and between the trades installing them – are everyday occurrences. Equally common is the hopeless entanglement of sub-systems that results from leaving placement of building parts to the means and methods of each successive trade. Piping and cabling are typically entangled and stuffed into wall cavities and floor-ceiling assemblies. This also makes renovation an unpredictable, chaotic and risky undertaking.

Environmental design plays out in three-dimensional space involving many actors. As it does so, grids become as basic a tool to interaction as the chess board is to chess players or harmonic scales are to musicians.[2] Such issues, although technical in nature, are entirely questions of design.

As is the case for all methodological tools, the need for grids becomes apparent once the distribution of design control is recognized.

●━●━●

Methodological sophistication is also required to recognize the role of horizontal themes in vertical design – for instance, how choosing

a given type on one level influences the character of design on
another. Urban designers in the Renaissance had little problem
imagining the buildings that would be found along the streets
they laid out. Each urban fabric was well known. It was stable
and vernacular, and therefore not subject to self-conscious invention or variable social preference. Innate typological knowledge
guided urban decisions about the block sizes and lot widths and
depths. Stable lower-level convention allowed urban design to
invent with confidence geometric patterns of streets and squares
never before seen.

Today the anticipated building typology is a variable to be
settled as part of the higher-level urban design task. In the same
way, the architect who designs a base building for lower-level fit-out
must understand what thematic deployment to expect there.
Decisions as to bay width, position, size and frequency of shafts
and ducts or plenums and, most importantly, public circulation,
must be made on the basis of assumptions of lower-level typology.
Law offices, research laboratories, festival market places, single
room occupancies, homes for extended families and live/work
studios may require different bay sizes, circulation patterns, entry
sequences, lighting and ventilation. Local habits and customs need
their own context. In short, typological expectations inform higher-
level architecture.

Yet such lower-level typologies are far from self-evident in
contemporary practice. In designing "open" plans for speculative
office, shopping mall or residential base buildings, the nature and
functional requirements of future tenants may be uncertain. In
leaving lower-level parties space for inhabitation, absent any
fixed floor plan, how does one compare alternative base building
proposals to determine the best design? Certain circulation
principles – such as the double-loaded corridor or the elevator
lobby – combined with specific dimensions, supporting structure

and utility distribution, imply certain types of inhabitation. But in seeking to technically describe such implications, our methodological means remain primitive.

The question is one of capacity. The concept is innate. Potential home buyers enter a room and immediately size it up, assessing its capacity to serve as a study, perhaps doubling as a guest room or play room. Base building developers and their investors need to evaluate leasing alternatives. What range of law offices, boutiques or apartments will a design accommodate? When a core tenant leaves, will the floor plate be easily reconfigured or subdivided to suit other kinds of tenants? In other words, what lower-level design does the higher level allow?

In urban design the question of capacity is no less relevant. The typological elements of the architecture intended to fill in the urban structure, and the urban structure's capacity to incorporate them, similarly need to be defined. On each level of environmental intervention, considerations of capacity must guide design. The emergence of capacity analysis as a formal tool is one result.

●●●

In other professions, ways of working – methodology – form part of a larger common body of knowledge. Mastery of that body of knowledge is a prerequisite for developing professional expertise. Medical students must know physics, chemistry, anatomy and analytical and hands-on diagnostic methods and the workings of the human body and its component systems before they swear the Hippocratic oath and can be entrusted with healing others. Law students immerse themselves in the body of law and precedent, and become officers of the court. Engineers must know the strengths and behavior of materials and how forces act upon them before being licensed to design.

Yet little common knowledge of the structure and behavior of our environmental fields or how to practice in them unites the architectural profession. We devote years to learning to shape architectural form but barely skim the surface of the fields to which our architecture will contribute. Schools, licensing boards, professional organizations and publications continually and conditionally redefine built environment in different ways at different times and locations to the point where, in contrast to other professions, we have almost no agreed upon shared core body of knowledge.

Clearly, the architectural profession's failure to share a common environmental body of knowledge has profound implications. It perpetuates our unsupported belief that environment is somehow the product of architectural design, rather than a complex and autonomous entity, to whose well-being we may contribute by design and whose ways we need to understand.[3]

If a common language is a secondary characteristic of a profession, there again, architecture is an exception. Precise vocabularies and jargon describe the human body, the law and jurisprudence and the principles of applied physics. Architects, however, tend to present, discuss and defend projects in the idiosyncratic language of critics, steeped in phenomenology, personal meaning and poetic experience. Design instructors and writers on architecture take pride in coining uniquely personal ways to describe environment that stand out from the usages of their peers. A common professional language to research and report on environment in terms of architecture need not eliminate poetic expression in favor of technical jargon, but it would establish separate, more general terms of reference with which to build knowledge.

As in medicine, we must first do no harm. Once we agree to become students of environmental form, we may not only succeed in improving it, but in building a foundation on which a successful contemporary profession can be grounded.

To understand environment, we must first ask what is general and normative prior to considering what is exceptional. When architects seek to heal and enhance the thematic and the commonplace, in a world where sculptural design of free-standing buildings is no longer the primary focus of the profession, the history of architecture as a collection of extraordinary works of art becomes of secondary importance.

In this view, architectural and urban historiography acquire new roles. Historiography, as we know it, developed when traditions of type, technology and style grew meaningless and Modernism therefore chose to re-invent environment. The historiography of the ordinary field, however, is yet to be written. It might well reveal, in the last century or two, the quiet but steady establishment of new thematic qualities, new common elements and new conventions of horizontal and vertical interaction. It is upon such conventions that the present century now builds. Such common features may well prove more important for the future of our fields than our most sacred and celebrated architectural monuments and icons.

Our return to the field makes for a mixture of the vernacular and the professional. This may render the former obsolete and the latter in need of redefinition. In the perspective of environmental history, we find ourselves at the end of five centuries of Albertian self-reference. Post-modernism may represent a phase of transition towards a new, not yet fully understood professionalism.

Styles, systems and other social preferences used to identify an architect. They have now become variables, alternatives to be appropriated from place to place, commodities within a global marketplace of ideas and values that no longer bind the profession. In their place, a shared body of knowledge and methods must define architecture as they define all professions. These are the well-springs of our art and our science, and what ultimately renders the joy of creation.

●●●

Knowledge of the field further suggests that architecture education must be re-examined. Our ways of teaching and learning design stem from a time when the field was not yet a problem, nor even a fit subject for Architecture; a time when master building, engineering and design at all scales could be encompassed in the expertise of a single profession. Architects form their lifelong values in the design studio. Its teaching format – a by-product of the French Revolution – serves the Palladian role model. Studio-based education assumes that design is about total control of a discrete and self-contained building. As such, there is little place for distributing design, collaboration or hands-on dialogue with the field.

It may be that the studio format with its intimate and ritualistic interaction between master and apprentice is essential to acquire and internalize the hands-on guild training of design. But further assumptions – that this is a sufficient design foundation for contemporary architects; that it is the best or only way to acquire design skills to serve the long-term needs of built environment, and thus of the profession – must be challenged. Studio training does not prepare architects to work in a field where each intervention is one among many, where design must be shared and coordinated. Neither the purpose of the mainstream architecture curriculum, nor the studio format, nor its design discourse situates the act of designing in the living field.

An architecture of the field demands serious reconsideration of educational habits. Curricula must surely provide environments where architects learn the conventional ability to invent form in response to predetermined function and program. But building to provide continuity in space and enable transformation over time requires new knowledge and new skills. To learn this, students must become familiar with the overlapping physical, territorial and social orders of everyday environment; and learn how they are generated by levels, by construction, by control and by convention. They must learn how to handle form thematically; how to design with architectural systems; and how to design for growth and change. Curricula must incorporate thematic rule making; spatial coordination of sub-systems; general principles of design distribution; principles of design team management. The art of parsing and managing multi-level design tasks – like integrating and conducting voices within a musical score – needs to be recognized and studied as an advanced design skill.

●●●

To understand this in turn requires further knowledge of the historiography and fundamentals of field architecture. More than documentation of what is unique and ingenious and never before seen, it requires observation and understanding of what is shared and how it has evolved over time. The extraordinary can only be understood in the context of the ordinary. In the past, this was self-evident. But where the ordinary is no longer self-evident, a new approach is in order.

The study of architectural form as an artistic invention has been the focus of courses in theory. The general study of environmental form as an autonomous body must be added to it.[4] To the extent that fields are about intervention and change, we need to understand the history of environmental form from that perspective. To the extent that it is about everyday environment, we need a history of common environmental forms: of types, patterns and systems and their shifts and transformations through time.

Our return to the field does not require that we abandon what we have acquired. It does make us aware of so much more we must learn to succeed in these new and challenging circumstances. Such an education would help to bridge the chasm between school and practice. It would provide an appropriate body of knowledge, and a sound theoretical base for the exercise of architecture. But it would extract such knowledge and such theory first of all from the experience of practice in the field.

About an attitude
in making architecture

SEVEN

The growth of the good in the world partly depends on acts
that do not enter history: we are better off than we might
have been thanks to the number of people living faithfully
in obscurity.

— George Eliot, *Middlemarch*

In the days of heroic modernism's naïve hopes and massive interventions, architects and critics who called attention to everyday and
ordinary environment tended to proffer social – or moral – reasons
for their bias. They held that human habitat deserves the architect's
devotion for humanitarian reasons, that the profession has an
obligation to shelter the masses and accommodate daily life.

   Such solemn trust is not exclusive to architecture – it applies to
all professions. The impact of professional power on contemporary
society is substantial. It is not always beneficial. Yet the topic of
these essays is the substance of architecture as a discipline. I have
thus contemplated the profession's disengagement from the field
and its inevitable return in terms of necessity and skills rather than
moral obligation: we need the field more than it needs us.

   There is a widespread and longstanding assumption that the
health and vigor of environmental fields depend on the genius and
talent of the professional designer. This is refuted by much that we

7.1–7.4 The primary task of architecture is to enhance human dignity

7.1 Rotterdam, Bergpolder apartment block, 1932–4, by Willem van Tijen, Brinkman and van der Vlugt.

7.2 Mass housing in Berlin.

7.3 Housing in Alexandria, Egypt, ca. 1970.

7.4 Housing in the environs of Rio de Janeiro, Brazil, ca. 1970.

observe, including the sheer complexity of the contemporary metropolis,[1] the proliferation of suburbia and the uncontrolled tenacity of the informal sector throughout the world.

It is seductive to believe that fields somehow need us, and to couch architectural practice in terms of a higher calling. But it is better to ask what the professional designer can uniquely contribute to the field's well-being. And, in fact, to the credit of many unsung colleagues and to the benefit of uncounted inhabitants, the profession has over time produced a substantial portfolio of everyday architecture of unobtrusive dignity and high quality.

If we do not exaggerate our importance and impact on environment, we cannot blame ourselves too much for the environmental failure we daily observe. Nonetheless, some of the dysfunction we witness does result from a combination of architecture ideology and ignorance of the ways of the field.

◉◉◉

Not long ago, I visited a new neighborhood under construction in Amsterdam. Publications were already praising its low-rise high-density fabric. It represented a return to public space formed by street walls.

In front of one entry, I came upon a resident on her hands and knees. She was busily tearing out newly-installed paver bricks, in order to plant shrubs in front of the floor-to-ceiling clear glazed panel at her entry. That glazing at her front door was all that separated inside from outside. She knew some mediating and identifying element was missing.

Nor, as it turned out, was she alone. In many parts of the neighborhood, wall-to-wall carpet in bedrooms and living rooms is separated from the concrete of the public sidewalk only by a floor-to-ceiling sheet of transparent glass. Shrubs and plants quickly

7.5 Amsterdam, Borneo Island residential neighborhood façades, 2003. Glass panes without mediating articulation separate living spaces from the sidewalk.

appear to mediate between private interior and public exterior. Curtains inside remain permanently drawn.

Similar instances abound in the design of contemporary housing. The absence of forms that mediate between public and private, and between inside and outside, does not result solely from contemporary architecture's predilection for sparseness and abstraction. It is yet another result of ignorance among the profession of what has always made fields work and stems from a lack of interest in human territorial needs. Throughout environmental history, those fundamental needs had provided one of the most prolific sources of architectural expression.

A convincing embodiment of that ignorance is found in the celebrated Amsterdam School façades. The designers' architectural articulation in that demonstration of architectural exuberance was dexterous. But it was also purely formal, and only skin deep. It dealt with profiles, rooflines and corners, with marvelous details of brickwork and carpentry. Yet all this compulsive form-making had little to do with mediating between private life inside and public space beyond. There are few forms of transition in the Amsterdam

7.6 Berlage extension of Amsterdam, "Amsterdam School" doors, 1930s. Front doors open directly onto the sidewalk without mediating articulation.

school street walls, doorways where the threshold butts directly against the sidewalk are frequent. The walls are elaborate urban screens, projecting to the public realm an image of layered richness, yet they are utterly devoid of territorial meaning.

Zones of transition have long been a hallmark of Western civic urban space. The sunken "area" of Georgian London townhouses, separating sidewalk and façade, is traversed by a bridge extending from sidewalk to entry door, lined with wrought iron banisters. Shallow front gardens in Boston's Back Bay similarly provide a zone that is thematically elaborated from house to house. Historic canal houses in Amsterdam provide a compressed zone of transition no more than four feet deep. It is composed of several elements in conjunction: stone slabs and short bollards mark it, stoops ascend at each door and steps descend to basements.

While each culture articulates this zone of transition in its own way, mediation between private and public is intrinsic to all vernacular architecture. In the natural history of fields, streets did not always connect town houses. They often linked large gated compounds for extended families or feudal communities gathered

7.7 London "areas"   **7.8** Boston Back Bay gardens   **7.9** Amsterdam stoops

around the residing lord. There, architectural elaboration turned inward and territory was treated in a defensive way with only the gate relating public and private space.

The Chinese family compound of several courtyards formed by pavilions under curved roofs was situated behind a blind wall at the street, punctuated by a gate. Arab Islamic urban fabric similarly keeps its riches inward: rooms open to courtyards for ventilation and light, but blind walls run along public space. The Pompeiian house placed a solitary gate on the street; its atrium remained hidden behind shops and blind walls. The Parisian fabric likewise follows a pattern of living around a courtyard, its gate now jealously guarded day and night by a concierge.

In most of the world throughout history, public space constituted dangerous space from which private life needed to be protected. Yet even in the most austere territorial conditions, forms of transition received architectural attention. The Chinese gate to the street was richly carved and roofed, with a decorated niche at the opposite alley wall. In its connection to the courtyard, the Arab Islamic entrance gate led to intermediate space: the path of the visitor was turned sideways to preserve privacy. The Parisian courtyard gate frames views into the semi-private yard. [Fig. 3.7]

Walled-in streets are not just an historic phenomenon. To this day, squatters in Latin America tend first to build a wall around their territory with a gate to the street. Only afterwards are rooms roofed within. [Fig. 3.4]

Suburban North America created an opposing trend: even where houses were a few steps apart, they behaved as if situated in an empty plain. Fences were considered un-neighborly. Consequently, territorial boundaries between lawns were clearly seen only when grass was mowed. The habit was once all-pervasive, but its limitations have become apparent. Fences and hedgerows now tend to subsequently appear around backyards and sideyards. Throughout the United States, walled and gated community compounds are restoring historic patterns of territorial demarcation with a vengeance.

Nevertheless, on the North American continent for a few generations, there was a promise of freedom and security in the public realm. Homes would need no marked boundaries, territories would require no protection. Cars remained unlocked. The suburban image of freedom and security strongly reinforced both the Palladian ideal of the villa and also the architect's vision of boundless space flowing freely between inside and outside. This vision still guides much of our design; and in its thrall the memory of forms of transition faded as historic evidence of them grew somehow pale, invisible.

The articulation of spatial transition, of inside and outside, built and not built, has always been central to architecture, tied as it was to territorial meaning. The assertion of inhabitation by way of gates, boundaries, walls, hedges or fences, plantings or pavement, or simply a stone placed along a path, has for millennia been the essence of place-making and the beginning of spatial definition. But no longer. Modern architecture, obsessed with the formal ideal of free flowing space, abhorred barriers. The ideal was expressed in the building on *pilotis* with a public lawn flowing underneath.

The sources of such reductive innovation are complex. We can be certain, however, that they do not represent a sudden fundamental change in human need for spatial control as it has developed over thousands of years. The absence of territorial articulation in contemporary architecture reflects neither the territorial reality of our cities nor the territorial instincts of their inhabitants. Our fundamental need for safety and control continues unabated.

Contemporary urban environment is replete with lines we may or may not cross: There are "no man's land" boundaries around some neighborhoods, there remain parking lot and garage barriers, and apartment building entries. There are lobbies, elevators, stairways and public or semi-public access corridors. Ultimately, there are the doors that give onto single apartments, houses and work places.

Gates and boundaries have always been a source of architectural elaboration. No longer. While they still function and multiply, they now tend to be marked in a technical – rather than architectural – way. At any point along our path, we may be called upon to push buttons or insert or swipe access cards, to wait for mechanical or human responses, for booms to raise and doors or gates to swing, slide or silently click open. We may be aware of cameras recording our presence or electronic devices that monitor movement, light, body heat or sound. All of this remains architecturally unexpressed, if not invisible.

Meanwhile, architecture more often than not insists on preserving the appearance of free flowing space. The glass wall thus cuts across our path of movement until, as we approach, a hidden eye opens the glass panel that does not really want to be there.

Architects need not copy the walls and gates of historic environment. But as long as we ignore territorial reality and its many degrees and devices of public/private transition, environment remains untrue, human dignity is not fully served and architecture is deprived of a vital source of inspiration. Our return to the field will be marked, eventually, by the degree to which we recapture this rich and ancient art.

◖◗◖◗◖◗

Our return to the field is not just marked by forgotten reality. There is also a new one: the global culture of which we are part poses a problem without much precedent. To be sure, architecture, distinct from local fields and sustained by a network, has a long history. Architecture has often traveled to be inserted in foreign fabric. Romans built their barracks, palaces, courthouses, villas and residences, as well as entire new towns, throughout the empire's territory. Emulated by local elites, they eventually might add to local vernacular. Vestiges of Roman urbanism can still be traced in Mediterranean fabrics. They are still uncovered when bulldozers make way for new interventions as far North of Rome as Great Britain and the Netherlands. Earlier, in the same way, the Greeks had left their mark on far-flung places around the Mediterranean and beyond.

Much later, Palladian architecture was embedded in the vernacular fields of diverse cultures spanning across a large part of the globe. This time the network architecture did not represent an intrusion into the local by foreign power but rather an elite of privilege, wealth and knowledge, whose members shared education, taste and manners across national boundaries. Still later, the International Style also broadcast its products across local fields, but it had a narrower, predominantly artistic and intellectual *avant garde* base. With the gradual re-entry of the profession into the common field, this base evaporated. In contrast to historic examples, today's global architecture does not insert itself for cohabitation with autonomous and living local fabric but tends to transform or replace that fabric itself. This is a case without precedent.

Today, wherever we work, architects have no informed attitude toward the local. What we call contemporary architecture is the product of a highly networked international professional culture. Its members attend similar schools and read similar publications. Nevertheless, although we still look over our shoulder for approval within that global peer group, the profession's claim to any universal symbolic meaning has long been abandoned. In spite of its dazzling haute couture design output, on the whole, the profession no longer has anything particular to say about architectural form.

Perhaps that is just as well. There cannot be similar fields in all corners of the world; style cannot frame an international profession. With respect to the architect's environmental mission, inventing form and setting trends are no longer of the essence. The new game, which is not driven by style, remains obscured by the profession's vestigial self-absorption. Having abandoned a common style, we are still consumed with developing a personal style that can be legitimated by extensive publication among our peers.

Nevertheless, local spirit of place can neither be globalized nor personalized. And it is the local that the contemporary practitioner is expected to enhance, precisely because it is irreplaceable and unique. How can a globally sophisticated profession improve local fields? That question leads to another: What do architects as a profession hold in common, now that style is no longer of the essence? The answer is knowledge and method.

●●●

Global knowledge of environmental form now passes to client and user as a commodity, devoid of architectural meaning. Contemporary typologies such as the apartment building, the office tower and the shopping mall are globally shared. But they no longer represent any particular culture. Although Asians, Middle Easterners and Europeans may denounce globalization as American cultural imperialism, such building types have become universal elements of contemporary life, no longer foreign to any culture.

This does not necessarily presage a uniform global environment. Contrary to what the professional traveler who visits only airports, offices and hotel rooms abroad may think, it opens these building forms to local interpretation and elaboration. In a global culture, it may still make sense to invest in an architect whose personal signature lends instant brand name recognition and added value. But simultaneously, in various parts of the world, leading architects are seeking an ethnic or traditional local signature, even in the design of skyscrapers.

More and more local authorities, equally informed on the global state of the art, invite foreign architects not to contradict the local field, but to enhance it and push it forward. In other words, local clients have begun to employ the international network of architects for their own purposes, to inspire architects of international stature. Architecture still travels, but the conditions have changed. Increasingly, the challenge is no longer to pose an alternative imported from afar, it is to intelligently engage in a dialogue with what is there.

Outside the bounds of formal architecture, but no less important, new local typologies that represent neither extensions of traditional vernacular nor responses to international trends have begun to arise as well. Examples include a new kind of combined small factory surmounted by a family residence as reported by

7.10 Dammam, Saudi Arabia, 1980s. A new villa typology emerging.

Ming-Hung Wang in Taiwan,[2] and an entirely new kind of sumptu-
ous villa – walled and gated – observed by Jamel Akbar in Saudi
Arabia. Similar typological innovations are taking root all over the
world, yet they remain largely undocumented because they are not
recognized as Architecture.

The model of an international *avant garde* forged by heroic
modern architects a century ago has run its course. In today's
kaleidoscopic situation, its adherents are preoccupied with formal
criticism and publication, still believing that globalism lends
exclusivity. Such self-referential discourse has become increasingly
irrelevant. To be sure, our design expertise, if we manage to explicate
it, will continue to be globally applicable, but our architectural
styles are not. Local field conditions are likely to gradually come
into their own precisely because connecting to the global network
has grown mundane: it no longer conveys power or prestige.

◗◗◗

Well-informed citizens, while invoking international standards and
cutting-edge technology, are no longer overwhelmed by foreign
credentials or portfolios. Any architect they select, local or foreign,

while fully cognizant of global state of the art, must understand their immediate values and preferences.

Ironically, within extremely globalized society, local identity is priceless. But for globally informed clients, identification with the local is not necessarily identification with the past. Nor need it represent sentimental or theme park regionalism. It may well shape an entirely new kind of field.

For the de-localized resident who works as part of a network – whose roots and relatives lie elsewhere, and who shares neither hobbies, nor ethnic background, nor religion nor personal history with neighbors – physical neighborhood, local environment and income level may provide the only common bonds. Why live then in a place with no identity? In the future, neighborhoods may have architectures in which both regional and global influences are apparent, but which nonetheless have profound identity.

A profession needs a common base. If style no longer binds architecture and nor do material or systems preferences, what will hold it together? Self-expression does not produce something that can be shared among peers. But architects, like agriculturists and other professionals, may globally share knowledge, methodology and skills, whose application is determined by local conditions. This sets the architect free to honor a field's characteristics and make it bloom.

The architect is ultimately a visitor invited to join in an ongoing environmental conversation. Architecture as an art of conversation is the essence of thematic design. In all social intercourse, human beings instinctively pick up clues and shape their acts accordingly. The ability is universal: we use words and phrases to signal our belonging. We read body language and respond in kind. To show who we are to the circle within which we want to be, we must first gain admission. We must establish a common background. Against that backdrop, individual contributions can be recognized:

Conformity on some levels is the prerequisite for individual expression of identity.

In other times, subject, tone and nuance differed from one exclusive salon to another. Visitors might arrive from abroad or from next door, attend frequently or as one-time guests. Conversation tested and showcased wit, intelligence, talent and judgment. The unwritten rule of the game was obeyed by all: the individual's desire to shine must never overpower the general purpose, which was to make the salon, the event and the conversation brilliant. The vainglorious, the dimwitted and the boorish received the cold shoulder.

Conversation occurs in a specific locale. It is place-bound. To converse is to share real space with others and let personal chemistry, body language, spatial and ambient qualities, décor, food and drinks all contribute to the interaction. Conversation is quite different from networked communication and exchange. For the latter, we remain separated in space while conveying thoughts, opinions and designs via various media. Threaded conversation, instant messaging, instant imaging and other forms of mediated exchange do not alter this fundamental condition. They no more represent *in situ* face-to-face conversation than do phone calls, letters or faxes. They allow opinion to be voiced without space being shared. Conversation does not.

Buildings, like individuals, can be linked by social networks and grouped according to "schools" or "movements." Critics rightly observe how buildings or architectural events in one part of the world influence the character of buildings elsewhere. But a conversation among buildings requires that they inhabit the same space and relate to one another three-dimensionally in a common landscape.

In that conversation, the attitude of the designer, rather than local origin, is what counts. The practitioner may, like Bramante in Todi, decline to enter into local conversation, opting instead to make a statement to impress peers elsewhere in the network culture. The visiting practitioner may engage what is there – respecting local environmental themes, seeking to enhance their elaboration and adding quality to the space buildings share. Or he may, like Palladio in Venice, establish a counterpoint within a strong and coherent extant fabric.

Acts of conversation must contribute to the whole, enriching the theme at hand or bringing to light new aspects of meaning. In all cases, mutual understanding is a prerequisite.

There is no reason to assume that conversation is intrinsically opposed by talent or by signature work. In realizing the DG Bank Building in Berlin, Frank Gehry abandoned his customary mono-logue to enter into a textbook example of dialogue with the field. Gehry responded to urban bylaws with sublime proportions and exemplary sensitivity. The building's outward restraint enhances the mysterious presence of the signature conference space inside.

The architect, as a contemporary professional, is increasingly a visitor, a foreigner. This demands a higher degree of sophistication than any historic example of the architect's role can teach. As it gradually becomes the norm, the mastery of thematic arts will be a basic requirement for all practitioners.

●━●━●

The visitor is not alone in requiring conversational skills. Those who structure must be equally sensitive to exchange among forms. Old-fashioned urban design, the laying out of streets, squares and house lots, is the most familiar example. But the most noble and generous of environmental acts – providing structure – is not restricted to the urban scale. It occurs on all levels of environment, from the layout of rooms to the layout of urban fabric. Design on a

it and the vision and personality to lead peers to cooperate and achieve it.

●●●

After a lapse of several generations, thematic design has begun to resurface in new ways, as environment comes into its own in new times. The first steps may appear tentative, the methods experimental and the results of mixed quality. But unmistakably, practice is once more forging ahead of theory and education, driven by the realities of our global society.

The synergy between participants in environmental conversation creates a game with its own rules. The game may be largely implicit, but it must be played with conviction. The very implicitness of the exchange is its strength. Theory and method will follow, but the privilege of practice is to nurture, by patient transformation rather than willful exception, what is new and promising, and already taking root in the field.

Towards an architecture of the field

Study the field:
It will be there without you; you can contribute to it.
Study the field as a living organism.
It has no form, but it has structure. Find its structure and form
    will come.

The field has continuity.
Merge with it and others will join you.
Because the field has continuity:
No job is large or small: all that you do adds to the field.

No one builds alone:
When you do something large, leave the small to others.
When you do something small, enhance the large.
Respond to those before you:
When you find structure, inhabit it;
When you find type, play with it;
When you find patterns, seek to continue them.

Be hospitable to those after you:
Give structure as well as form.
The more you seek to continue what was done by others,
    the more you will be recognized for it:
The more others will continue what you did.

Cooperate:
When you can borrow from others borrow, and praise them for it.
When you can steal from others steal, and admit it freely.
No matter what you do, your work will be your own.

Avoid style:
Leave it to critics and historians.

Choose method:
It is what you share with your peers.

Forget self-expression:
It is a delusion.
Whatever you do will be recognized as your expression;
      don't give it a second thought.

Do what the field needs.

Quantity	Product Details
1	**Palladio's Children [Paperback] [2005] Habraken, N.J.** **SKU:** 0P-PGGK-BCDM **ASIN:** 0415357918 **Listing ID:** 1122OP2IPT2 **Order Item ID:** 41008839382427 **Condition:** Used - Good **Comments:** Appears unread.Text tight and clean.Minor shelf wear bumps to covers.

0.2   Villa Rotonda, view from portico.

Notes

ONE Palladio's Children

1   Andrea Palladio, *The Four Books on Architecture* [*Quattro libri dell' architettura*], trans. Robert Tavernor and Richard Schofield, Cambridge, MA: MIT Press, 1997.

2   Adolf K. Placzek, Foreword to *Sebastian Serlio on Domestic Architecture: The Sixteenth-Century Manuscript of Book IV*, Cambridge, MA: MIT Press, 1978, p. 7.

3   Adolf K. Placzek, introduction to Andrea Palladio, *The Four Books of Architecture*, New York: Dover Publications, 1965, p. vi.

4   *Le Corbusier et son atelier rue de Sèvres 35, Œuvres Complètes 1910–1965. vols I–VII*. Zurich: Les Éditions d'Architecture, various dates.

5   Camillo Semenzato, *The Rotonda of Andrea Palladio*. vol. I, *corpus palladianum*, trans. Ann Percy, University Park, PA: Pennsylvania State University Press, 1968, p. 24. Semenzato reports vestiges of a second, pedestrian approach in the axis perpendicular to the first, to which it was actually connected. Whereas the road makes a right angle turn, the path maintained the building in full view the entire way, and would have offered the visitor a less anchored vista.

6   Ibid. "It is not conceivable that . . . entrances were planned at the southeast and southwest. From these points the terracing drops too rapidly; besides, service passages leading toward the fields and woods were opened under the two staircases."

7   Wright builds just below the crest of the hill, to marry the building into the slope.

8   To the consternation of architects and critics, Le Corbusier later betrayed these principles in the chapel of Notre-Dame-du-Haut (Ronchamp, France) and subsequently in the design of the Convent of La Tourette (Eveux-sur-Arbresle, France).

9   See Chapter 1, "Memoria et Prudentia: Patrician Mentalities and res aedificatori" in Manfredo Tafuri, *Venice and the Renaissance*, Cambridge, MA: MIT Press, 1989, pp. 1–13.

10 The new network culture, to which Palladio gave such powerful impetus, arose in Italy but later emanated directly from the British Isles. Introduced by Inigo Jones and brought to a culmination by Christopher Wren, neo-classical treatment of houses for the new middle class became part and parcel of the building trade. Its development was also strongly influenced by father and son Woods, the Adams brothers, and particularly aided by pattern books of all kinds. In the terraced houses of Georgian London, Palladian elements eventually came to constitute what might be termed a new vernacular.

11 The term *international style* was popularized by publication of Henry Russell-Hitchcock, Jr. and Philip Johnson, *The International Style: Architecture since 1922*, New York: W. W. Norton, 1932, subsequent to the famous New York Museum of Modern Art exhibition.

12 The network that formed around the International Style was predominantly professional. Groups such as the Bauhaus lacked the broad political and financial authority, appeal and patronage of classicism and were frequently dependent on the support of local individuals.

13 Particularly in their writings in Le Corbusier, *Vers une Architecture*, Paris: G. Crès, 1923, and in the magazine *L'Esprit Nouveau* (1918–25).

14 John Julius Norwich, *A History of Venice*, New York: Knopf, 1982, p. 389.

15 Howard Burns in collaboration with Lynda Fairbairn and Bruce Boucher, *Andrea Palladio, 1508–1580: The Portico and the Farmyard: Catalogue*, London: Arts Council of Great Britain, 1975, p. 9.

16 Ibid., p. 12.

17 Manfred Wundram, Thomas Pape and Martin Paolo, *Andrea Palladio, 1508–1580*, Köln: Benedikt Taschen, 1989, p. 8.

18 Andrea Palladio (1508–1580) was born in Padua. He began his career as an apprentice stonemason and was initiated into the stonemason's guild in 1524 in Vicenza. There he met his benefactor, Gian Giorgio Trissino, who underwrote his travel to Rome and study of antique architecture. His first important work as an architect was rebuilding the "basilica" (town hall and market) in Vicenza; most of his subsequent work was in the Vicenza area. Palladio's renowned country villas were built mainly in the 1550s and 1560s, followed by urban *palazzi* in

Vicenza. Work on the church of San Giorgio Maggiore in Venice began in 1565, followed by the commission for the Villa Rotonda in 1566. In 1570, the year *Quattro libri dell'architettura* was published, Palladio moved his household to Venice. In 1576, the first stone was laid for the Church of the Redentore in Venice. See Paul Holberton, *Palladio's Villas: Life in the Renaissance Countryside*, London: J. Murray, 1990, p. 65.

19 Malraux introduced the similar concept of the *musée imaginaire* in André Malraux, *Les voix du silence*, Paris: NRF, 1953.

20 In commending Alberti's *De Re Aedificatoria* to the great patron Lorenzo the Magnificent, the fifteenth-century literary figure Angelo Poliziano [Angelo Ambrogini] comments, "his invention was not limited to machinery, lifts, and automata, but also included the wonderful forms of buildings." Leon Battista Alberti, *On the Art of Building in Ten Books [De Re Aedificatoria]*, trans. Joseph Rykwert, Neil Leach and Robert Tavernor. Cambridge, MA: MIT Press, 1996, p. 1.

21 John James, *Chartres, les constructeurs*, vols I–II, Chartres, France: Société Archéologique d'Eure-et-Loire, 1977–9. James's meticulous and well-documented study is devoted to identifying the various master builders involved in building the cathedral over the course of more than 40 building campaigns. See p. 91 for the identification of 15 teams. See also p. 11, where James observes that nine teams did the majority of the work.

22 This passage, of course, is inspired by Joseph Rykwert, *The Idea of a Town: The Anthropology of Urban Form in Rome, Italy and the Ancient World*, Cambridge, MA: MIT Press, 1995.

TWO Leaving the Field

1 John McAndrew, *Venetian Architecture of the Early Renaissance*, Cambridge, MA: MIT Press, 1980, p.195.

2 Tafuri, op. cit., p. 8.

3 Holberton, op. cit., p. 67.

4 The term *social memory* is endebted to the usage in Stanford Anderson, "Memory without monuments: vernacular architecture," *Traditional Dwellings and Settlements Review: Journal of the International Association for the Study of Traditional Environments*, vol. xi, no. 1, pp. 13–22. Anderson states, "I hypothesize that vernacular architecture, whether of preliterate or literate societies – and even what we know as the

'dwelling types' or 'urban fabric' of modern settlements – raise intrinsically interesting issues of architecture closely linked to memory."
p. 19.

5   Tafuri, op. cit., p. 10.

6   Leon Battista Alberti, op. cit.

7   Ibid., p. 3.

8   Geoffrey Scott first published *The Architecture of Humanism: A Study in
    the History of Taste* in 1914, (New York: Scribner, 1914). The term *age of
    humanism* and the prevailing view of an Italian Renaissance that placed
    the individual human being at center stage gained enormous cultural
    capital following the destruction of World War II. The broad influence
    of "L'Europe de la Renaissance: l'âge de l'humanisme," a pan-
    European art exhibition mounted in 1954, was followed in rapid suc-
    cession by: Rudolph Wittkower, *Architectural Principles in the Age of
    Humanism*, New York: Columbia University Studies, 1962; publication
    of the French Language catalogue, André Chastel and R. Klein,
    L'Europe de la Renaissance: L'âge de l'humanisme, Paris: Editions des
    Deux-Mondes, 1963; its rapid translation into English and many other
    languages; and the publication of Gerald Abraham, *The Age of
    Humanism, 1540–1630*, New York: Oxford University Press, 1968. By the
    time Wittkower's seminal publication appeared, the term age of
    humanism and its broader implications were implictly understood:
    they required and received no explanation.

9   Giorgio Vasari, *The Lives of the Artists*, trans. Julia Conaway Bondonella
    and Peter Bondonella, New York: Oxford University Press, 1991.

10 Alberti, op. cit., p. 3.

11 Ibid.

12 Arnaldo Bruschi, *Bramante*, London: Thames and Hudson, 1977, p.
    162. Bruschi includes the building in Bramante's *œuvre*, but adds that
    the attribution is undocumented. He also notes, "If the design of the
    Todi church did originate with him, it was certainly altered." Others
    have attributed the origin of the church to a variety of sources, includ-
    ing the master builder Cola di Caprarola. See, for instance, Michele
    Furnari, *Formal Design in Renaissance Architecture: From Brunelleschi to
    Palladio*, New York: Rizzoli, 1995, p. 32.

13 Contemporary sketches by Leonardo da Vinci portray a remarkably
    similar building. On a par with his explorations of machines and

human bodies, it is rendered as an object floating in space, unconnected to any site.

14 Alberti, op. cit., p. 140.

15 Ibid.

16 McAndrew, op. cit., p. 232. See also discussion of Santa Maria Formosa pp. 282, 285.

17 Alberti, op. cit., p. 7.

18 Ibid. Rykwert retains the original word in his translation, sometimes using *design* for reasons of clarity.

19 James V. Wertsch, *Voices of the Mind: A Sociocultural Approach to Mediated Action*, Cambridge, MA: Harvard University Press, 1991, p. 49. With respect to language, as Wertsch summarizes, in Bakhtin's view, "the notion of sole, isolated authorship is a bogus one . . . multiple authorship is a necessary fact about all texts, written or spoken."

THREE About Fields

1 McAndrew, op. cit., p. 195.

2 Christopher Alexander, Sara Ishikawa and Murray Silverstein with Max Jacobson, Ingrid Fiksdahl-King and Schlomo Angel, *A Pattern Language: Towns, Buildings, Construction*, New York: Oxford University Press, 1977.

3 Amos Rapoport, *House Form and Culture*, Englewood Cliffs, NJ: Prentice-Hall, 1969, p. 47: "My basic hypothesis, then, is that house form is . . . the consequence of a whole range of socio-cultural factors."

4 The term was first used in N. J. Habraken, "Forms of understanding: thematic knowledge and the modernist legacy," in Martha Pollak, ed., *The Education of the Architect: Historiography, Urbanism and the Growth of Architectural Knowledge*, Cambridge, MA, MIT Press, 1997. The underlying concept of forms of understanding was further developed in N. J. Habraken, *The Structure of the Ordinary: Form and Control in the Built Environment*, ed. Jonathan Teicher, Cambridge, MA: MIT Press, 1998. See in particular pp. 230, 308–10.

5 Lewis Mumford, *The City in History: Its Origins, its Transformations, and its Prospects*, London: Pelican Books, 1966, pp. 501–5.

6 See Dr. L. Jansen, "Derde Vergroting van Amsterdam [The Third Extension of Amsterdam]," in *52nd Yearbook of the Amstelodamum Society*, Amsterdam: J. H. de Bussy, 1959. Dr Jansen meticulously studied the

preserved minutes of the Amsterdam Town Council at the time. He found no evidence of any plan in the sense of a document as we would expect today. To proceed based on the town's familiar patterns required no "design." The council therefore devoted its deliberations to costs, dimensions and priorities. Jansen concludes: "It is as good as certain that the famous Plan of Three Canals never, in fact, existed."

7   See N.J. Habraken, *The Structure of the Ordinary*, op. cit., pp. 318–21 for further discussion of the third extension of Amsterdam.

8   David H. Pinkney, *Napoleon III and the Rebuilding of Paris*, Princeton, NJ: Princeton University Press, 1958, p. 213: "The rebuilding of Paris was controversial when it was in progress . . . the controversy goes on."

9   Julian Beinart, "Scacchiera ed economia nel XIX secolo = Grid and its application in the XIXth century city," *Spazio e Società*, vol. 20, no. 84, Oct.–Dec. 1998, pp. 60–71. Beinart credits Haussmann with the inventive application of deficit spending in anticipation of increased tax revenues that would offset long-term loans; he further notes that the loans in question were paid off only in 1929.

10   See also N. J. Habraken, *The Structure of the Ordinary*, op. cit., pp. 312–7.

11   John Charlewood Turner and William Mangin, "Dwelling Resources in South America," *Architectural Design*, vol. 33, August 1963, pp. 360–93; and John F.C. Turner, *Housing by People: Towards Autonomy in Building Environments*, New York: Pantheon Books, 1977. Turner was the first to point out the important role of squatters in providing a very large part of the world's housing. His initiative brought serious academic attention to "informal" building processes and eventually influenced World Bank policy.

12   Definitions of "informal" or "self-help" processes, and assessments of the vast numbers involved, differ widely. To cite several examples: Reinhard Goethert, *Kairo: Zur Leistungsfähigkeit: Inoffizieller Stadtrandentwicklung*, Köln: Deutscher Gemeindeverlag, 1986, p. 50, cites studies by Abt Associates, the World Bank and other agencies to conclude that the percentage of informal building in Cairo, Egypt must lie between 50 and 80 percent of extant housing volume. Nabeel Hamdi, *Housing Without Houses*, New York: Van Nostrand, 1991, p. 5, cites a 1987 *Global Report* to the effect that 40 percent of Mexico City, 60 percent of Bogota, 85 percent of Addis Ababa and 70 percent of Dar es Salaam are occupied by squatters and other informal settlements.

13 John W. Reps, *Cities of the American West: A History of Frontier Urban Planning*, Princeton, NJ: Princeton University Press, 1979, p. 71: "On April 22, 1889, at noon, the borders of the 'Unassigned Lands' were opened. Preceded by a number of 'sooners,' prospective settlers rushed in – in trains, carts, and carriages and on foot. On the first day, the town of Guthrie was no more than a field. Hundreds of individuals literally squatted on the ground, having staked their claims . . . Within a year, evidence of informal settlement had vanished . . . Guthrie and similar 'overnight cities' could not be distinguished from other Midwestern towns."

14 See Carl W. Condit, *The Rise of the Skyscraper*, Chicago: University of Chicago Press, 1952 and *The Chicago School of Architecture: A History of Commercial and Public Building in the Chicago area, 1875–1925*, Chicago: University of Chicago Press, 1964. Condit provides a detailed account of the developments after the great fire, of which this summary is an interpretation.

15 Gilbert Herbert and Sylvina Sosnovsky, *Bauhaus on the Carmel and the Crossroads of Empire: Architecture and Planning in Haifa during the British Mandate*, Jerusalem: Yad Izhak Ben-Zvi, 1993.

16 Among important exceptions are Frank Lloyd Wright and Bruce Goff, both of whom saw themselves as champions of suburban society. Wright published idealized suburban homes throughout his career, from model homes (*Ladies Home Journal*, 1900) to his subsequent Broadacre City and American System and Usonian houses. Virtually all of Bruce Goff's celebrated homes were, in location and ethos, resolutely, albeit oddly, suburban.

17 See also N. J. Habraken, *The Structure of the Ordinary*, op. cit., pp. 273–4.

FOUR Encounters with the Field

1 Tony Garnier, *Une Cité Industrielle: Étude pour la construction des villes*, Paris: Auguste Vincent, 1918. Subsequent editions include: Paris: C. Massin & Company, 1939, and, ed. Riccardo Mariani, New York: Rizzoli, 1990.

2 René Jullian, *Tony Garnier, constructeur et utopiste*, Paris: P. Sers, 1989, also covers his extensive career as a practicing architect in Lyon.

3 Ibid., p. 15.

4   See also Le Corbusier, *Vers Une Architecture*, nouvelle édition, Paris: Vincent, Freal & Compagnie, 1958, pp. 42–3.

5   Robert Venturi, *Complexity and Contradiction in Architecture*, New York: Museum of Modern Art, 1966.

6   Steen Eiler Rasmussen, *Experiencing Architecture*, trans. Eve Wendt, Cambridge, MA: Technology Press of the Massachusetts Institute of Technology and Wiley, 1959.

7   Camillo Sitte, *City Planning According to Artistic Principles*, trans. George R. Collins and Christiane Crasemann Collins, New York: Random House, 1965.

8   Colin Rowe and Fred Koetter, *Collage City*, Cambridge, MA: MIT Press, 1978.

9   Aldo Rossi, *The Architecture of the City*, trans. Diane Ghirardo and Joan Ockman, Cambridge, MA: MIT Press, 1984.

10 Giancarlo Cataldi, "From Muratori to Caniggia: the origins and development of the Italian school of design typology," *Urban Morphology: Journal of the International Seminar on Urban Form 2003*, vol. 7, no. 1, p. 23.

11 Robert Venturi, Denise Scott Brown and Steven Izenour, *Learning from Las Vegas: The Forgotten Symbolism of Architectural Form*, revised edition, Cambridge, MA: MIT Press, 1977.

12 See John F. Turner, *Housing by People*, op. cit., and John F. Turner, "Housing as a Verb," in eds John F. Turner and Robert Fichter, *Freedom to Build: Dweller Control of the Housing Process*, New York: Macmillan, 1972.

13 Jane Jacobs, *The Death and Life of Great American Cities*, New York: Random House, 1961.

14 Christopher Alexander *et al.*, op. cit.

15 Renée Y. Chow, *Suburban Space: The Fabric of Dwelling*, Berkeley: University of California Press, 2002.

16 Bernard Rudofsky, *Architecture Without Architects: A Short Introduction to Non-Pedigreed Architecture*, London: Academy Editions, 1964.

17 During a conference on housing typology in Korea, I noted an emerging architectural building type in which tightly huddled nuclear family dwellings employ traditional elements – compound walls, gates and blue-tiled roofs – while accommodating carports, state-of-the-art kitchens, bathrooms and air conditioning. Without a moment's hesitation, several colleagues replied, "That's not architecture." By implication, the line separating architecture and non-architecture is based on architectural vocabulary, and no self-respecting architect could design such houses. In fact, as is the case throughout the world, licensed architects can and do anonymously design such houses in response to client preferences. Nonetheless, local architects educated in a world-wide network had no problem identifying and agreeing on what is Architecture and what is not.

18   Robert Venturi, Denise Scott Brown and Steven Izenour, preface to *Learning from Las Vegas*, first edition, Cambridge, MA: MIT Press, 1972.

19   In the new preface to Robert Venturi, Denise Scott Brown and Steven Izenour, *Learning from Las Vegas: The Forgotten Symbolism of Architectural Form*, revised edition, Cambridge, MA: MIT Press, 1977, the authors state, "Las Vegas is not the subject of our book. The symbolism of architectural form is." Note also the new sub-title.

FIVE **Back in the Field Again**

1   The phrase, "long life, loose fit, low energy," has been attributed to Bob McLeod in Cambridge, England, in 1971. It was subsequently picked up and popularized in a number of contexts, notably in Alex Gordon, "Architects and Resource Conservation: the long life, loose fit, low energy study," *RIBA Journal*, January 1974, pp. 9–12. Loose fit was subsequently explored in a variety of contexts, including work by Simon Nicholson, John Turner and Colin Ward, and in single family dwellings in New Zealand by Edward Duc and Ian Carter.

2   N. J. Habraken, *The Structure of the Ordinary*, op. cit.

3   While estimates regarding the size of historical Greek towns vary, there is some consensus regarding the order of magnitude of their populations. Norman J. G. Pounds, "The urbanization of the classical world," *Ekistics*, vol. 31, Jan. 1971, pp. 22–35, calculates population on the basis of available food supply provided by arable land. This method has the advantage of accounting not only for the adult male population: it also factors in slaves, women and children. His calculations are based on study of the *polis*, a political unit that included attached rural population as well as the population dwelling within town walls. The Kalchidike peninsula yielded a range of from 100–4500 people per

polis, averaging perhaps 1800. Thus, many towns were the size of a large high-rise building. Pounds adds to his estimate a reference to Xenophon who "considered a city of 5000 a large one."

4   Martin Pawley, "The age of the serial identity building," *World Architecture*, no. 65, 1998, p. 26.

5   See, for instance, the Michael Graves façade redesign of the Ministry of Health, Welfare and Sport in the Hague, which was a scant three decades old.

6   Michael Dennis, *Court and Garden: From the French Hôtel to the City of Modern Architecture*, Cambridge, MA: MIT Press, 1986, pp. 86–7.

7   Hillary Ballon, *The Paris of Henry IV: Architecture and Urbanism*, Cambridge, MA: MIT Press, 1992.

8   For further discussion, see Gilbert Herbert, *The Dream of the Factory-Made House: Walter Gropius and Konrad Wachsmann*, Cambridge, MA: MIT Press, 1984.

9   Stephen Kendall and Jonathan Teicher, *Residential Open Building*, London: E & FN Spon, 2000, p. 263.

10   Shakespeare, *The Tragedy of Hamlet*, Act II, Scene II, Polonius's aside: "Though this be madness, yet there's method in't"

SIX Ways of Working

1   For related in-depth discussion of dominance, dependence and control distribution, see N. J. Habraken, *The Structure of the Ordinary*, op. cit., particularly pp. 30–8.

2   See Koos Bosma, Dorine van Hoogstraten and Martijn Vos, *Housing for the Millions: John Habraken and the SAR (1960–2000)*, Rotterdam: NAi Publishers, 2000, particularly pp. 219–28, for an introduction to the substantial body of research and design tools related to zones and margins and the "band grids" created under the aegis of the SAR [Architects' Research Foundation (1964–91)]. This research was based on a notion of modular coordination as a tool for coordinating the process of dimensioning, rather than enforcing standardized dimensions in repetitive modules.

3   N. J. Habraken, "Forms of understanding: thematic knowledge and the modernist legacy," in Martha Pollak, ed., *The Education of the Architect: Historiography, Urbanism and the Growth of Architectural Knowledge*, Cambridge, MA, MIT Press, 1997, pp. 267–293.

4   For a study of environmental form as an autonomous body, see N. J. Habraken, *The Structure of the Ordinary*, op. cit.

SEVEN About an Attitude in Making Architecture

1   See, for instance, Chuihua Judy Chung, Jeffrey Inaba, Rem Koolhaas, Sze Tsung Leong, eds, *Great Leap Forward: Harvard Design School Project on the City*, Cambridge, MA: Harvard Design School, 2001.

2   Ming-Hung Wang, "Factory-villa: a case of the emergence of type," *IAPS12 International Conference on Socio-Environmental Metamorphoses*, Proceedings IV, July 1992.

3   Spiro Kostof, *The City Shaped: Urban Patterns and Meanings through History*, Boston: Little, Brown and Co., 1991, pp. 121–2.

4   Walter Benjamin, *Das Passagen-Werk*, Chemnitz: Suhrkamp, 1982, a posthumous compilation of notes. See also Walter Benjamin, *The Arcades Project*, trans. Howard Eiland and Kevin McLaughlin, prepared on the basis of the German volume, ed. Rolf Tiedemann, Cambridge, MA : Harvard University Press, 1999.

5   Christian Norberg-Schulz, *Genius Loci: Towards a Phenomenology of Architecture*, New York: Rizzoli, 1980.

Select bibliography

Abraham, Gerald. *The Age of Humanism, 1540–1630*. New York: Oxford University Press, 1968.

Alberti, Leon Battista. *On the Art of Building in Ten Books* [*De Re Aedificatoria*], trans. Joseph, Rykwert, Neil, Leach and Robert, Tavernor, Cambridge, MA: MIT Press, 1996.

Alexander, Christopher, Ishikawa, Sara and Silverstein, Murray with Jacobson, Max, Fiksdahl-King, Ingrid and Angel, Schlomo. *A Pattern Language: Towns, buildings, construction*. New York: Oxford University Press, 1977.

Anderson, Stanford. "Memory without monuments: vernacular architecture," *Traditional Dwellings and Settlements Review: Journal of the International Association for the Study of Traditional Environments*, vol. xi, no. 1, pp. 13–22.

Ballon, Hillary. *The Paris of Henry IV: Architecture and Urbanism*. Cambridge, MA: MIT Press, 1992.

Beinart, Julian. "Scacchiera ed economia nel XIX secolo = Grid and its application in the XIXth century city," *Spazio e Società*, vol. 20, no. 84, Oct.–Dec. 1998, pp. 60–71.

Benjamin, Walter. *Das Passagen-Werk*, Chemnitz: Suhrkamp, 1982.

Bosma, Koos, van Hoogstraten, Dorine and Vos, Martijn. *Housing for the Millions: John Habraken and the SAR (1960–2000)*. Rotterdam: NAi Publishers, 2000.

Bruschi, Arnaldo. *Bramante*, London: Thames and Hudson, 1977.

Burns, Howard with Fairbairn, Lynda and Boucher, Bruce. *Andrea Palladio, 1508–1580: The Portico and the Farmyard:* catalogue. London: Arts Council of Great Britain, 1975.

Cataldi, Giancarlo. "From Muratori to Caniggia: the origins and development of the Italian school of design typology." *Urban Morphology: Journal of the International Seminar on Urban Form 2003*, vol. 7, no. 1, pp. 19–34.

Chastel, André and R. Klein. *L'Europe de la Renaissance: L'âge de l'humanisme*, Paris: Éditions des Deux-Mondes, 1963.

Chow, Renée Y. *Suburban Space: The Fabric of Dwelling*. Berkeley, CA: University of California Press, 2002.

Chung, Chuihua Judy, Inaba, Jeffrey, Koolhaas, Rem and Leong, Sze Tsung eds. *Great Leap Forward: Harvard Design School Project on the city*. Cambridge, MA: Harvard Design School, 2001.

Condit, Carl W. *The Rise of the Skyscraper*. Chicago: University of Chicago Press, 1952.

——. *The Chicago School of Architecture: A History of Commercial and Public Building in the Chicago Area, 1875–1925*. Chicago: The University of Chicago Press, 1964.

Dennis, Michael. *Court and Garden: From the French Hôtel to the City of Modern Architecture*. Cambridge, MA: MIT Press, 1986.

Furnari, Michele. *Formal Design in Renaissance Architecture: From Brunelleschi to Palladio*. New York: Rizzoli, 1995.

Garnier, Tony. *Une Cité Industrielle: Étude pour la construction des villes*. Paris: Auguste Vincent, 1918.

Goethert, Reinhard. *Kairo: Zur Leistungsfähigkeit: Inoffizieller Stadtrandentwicklung*, Köln: Deutscher Gemeindeverlag, 1986.

Gordon, Alex. "Architects and resource conservation: The long life, loose fit, low energy study," *RIBA Journal*, January 1974, pp. 9–12.

Habraken, N. J. "Cultivating the Field: About an attitude when making architecture," *Places* vol. 9, no. I (Winter 1994), pp. 8–21.

——. "Forms of understanding: thematic knowledge and the modernist legacy," in Martha Pollak, ed. *The Education of the Architect: Historiography, Urbanism and the Growth of Architectural Knowledge*. Cambridge, MA: MIT Press, 1997.

——. *The Structure of the Ordinary: Form and Control in the Built Environment*, Jonathan Teicher, ed. Cambridge, MA: MIT Press, 1998.

——. *Supports: An Alternative to Mass Housing*, second English edition, Jonathan Teicher, ed. London: Urban International Press, 1999.

Hamdi, Nabeel. *Housing Without Houses*. New York: Van Nostrand, 1991.

Herbert, Gilbert and Sosnovsky, Sylvina. *Bauhaus on the Carmel and the Crossroads of Empire: Architecture and Planning in Haifa during the British Mandate*. Jerusalem: Yad Izhak Ben-Zvi, 1993.

Holberton, Paul. *Palladio's Villas: Life in the Renaissance Countryside*. London: J. Murray, 1990.

Jacobs, Jane. *The Death and Life of Great American Cities*. New York: Random House, 1961.

James, John. *Chartres, les Constructeurs*, vols I–II. Chartres, France: Société Archaéologique d'Eure-et-Loire, 1977–9.

Jansen, Dr. L. "Derde Vergroting van Amsterdam [The Third Extension of Amsterdam]," *52nd Yearbook of the Amstelodamum Society*. Amsterdam: J. H. de Bussy, 1959.

Jullian, René. *Tony Garnier, constructeur et utopiste*. Paris: P. Sers, 1989.

Kendall, Stephen and Teicher, Jonathan. *Residential Open Building*. London: E & FN Spon, 2000.

Kostof, Spiro. *The City Shaped: Urban Patterns and Meanings through History*. Boston: Little, Brown and Co., 1991.

Le Corbusier *et al*. *Le Corbusier et son atelier rue de Sèvres 35, Œuvres Complètes 1910–1965*. vols. I–VII. Zurich: Les Éditions d'Architecture, various dates.

——. *Vers une Architecture*. Paris: Vincent, Freal & Compagnie, 1958.

McAndrew, John. *Venetian Architecture of the Early Renaissance*. Cambridge, MA: MIT Press, 1980.

Malraux, André. *Les voix du silence*. Paris: NRF, 1953.

Mumford, Lewis. *The City in History: Its Origins, its Transformations, and its Prospects*. London: Pelican Books, 1966.

Norberg-Schulz, Christian. *Genius Loci: Towards a Phenomenology of Architecture*. New York: Rizzoli, 1980.

Norwich, John Julius. *A History of Venice*. New York: Knopf, 1982.

Palladio, Andrea. *The Four Books on Architecture* [*Quattro libri dell' architettura*], trans. Robert Tavernor and Richard Schofield, Cambridge, MA: MIT Press, 1997.

Pawley, Martin. "The age of the serial identity building," *World Architecture*, no. 65, 1998, p. 26.

Pinkney, David H. *Napoleon III and the Rebuilding of Paris*. Princeton, NJ: Princeton University Press, 1958.

Placzek, Adolf K. "Introduction," Palladio, Andrea. *The Four Books of Architecture*, New York: Dover Publications, 1965.

——."Foreword," Serlio, Sebastian. *Sebastian Serlio on Domestic Architecture: The Sixteenth-Century Manuscript of Book IV.* Cambridge, MA: MIT Press, 1978.

Pounds, Norman J. G. "The urbanization of the classical world," *Ekistics*, vol. 31, Jan. 1971, pp. 22–35.

Rapoport, Amos. *House Form and Culture*. Englewood Cliffs, NJ: Prentice-Hall, 1969.

Rasmussen, Steen Eiler. *Experiencing Architecture*, trans. Eve Wendt, Cambridge, MA: Technology Press of the Massachusetts Institute of Technology and Wiley, 1959.

Reps, John W. *Cities of the American West: A History of Frontier Urban Planning*. Princeton, NJ: Princeton University Press, 1979.

Rossi, Aldo. *The Architecture of the City*, trans. Diane Ghirardo and Joan Ockman, Cambridge, MA: MIT Press, 1984.

Rowe, Colin and Koetter, Fred. *Collage City*. Cambridge, MA: MIT Press, 1978.

Rudofsky, Bernard. *Architecture Without Architects: A Short Introduction to Non-Pedigreed Architecture*. London: Academy Editions, 1964.

Russell-Hitchcock, Jr. Henry and Johnson, Philip. *The International Style: Architecture since 1922*. New York: W. W. Norton, 1932.

Rykwert, Joseph. *The Idea of a Town: the Anthropology of Urban Form in Rome, Italy and the Ancient World*. Cambridge, MA: MIT Press, 1995.

Scott, Geoffrey, *The Architecture of Humanism: A Study in the History of Taste*. New York: Scribner, 1914.

Semenzato, Camillo. *The Rotonda of Andrea Palladio*. vol. I, *corpus palladianum*, trans. Ann Percy, University Park, PA: Pennsylvania State University Press, 1968.

Sitte, Camillo. *City Planning According to Artistic Principles*, trans. George R. Collins and Christiane Crasemann Collins, New York: Random House, 1965.

Tafuri, Manfredo. *Venice and the Renaissance*. Cambridge, MA: MIT Press, 1989.

Turner, John F. C. "Housing as a verb," in Turner, John F. and Fichter, Robert eds. *Freedom to Build: Dweller Control of the Housing Process*, New York: Macmillan, 1972.

——. *Housing by People: Towards Autonomy in Building Environments*. New York: Pantheon Books, 1977

Turner, John F. C. and Mangin, William. "Dwelling resources in South America," *Architectural Design*, vol. 33, August 1963, pp. 360–93.

Vasari, Giorgio. *The Lives of the Artists*, trans. Julia Conaway Bondonella and Peter Bondonella. New York: Oxford University Press, 1991.

Venturi, Robert. *Complexity and Contradiction in Architecture*. New York: Museum of Modern Art, 1966.

Venturi, Robert, Scott Brown, Denise and Izenour, Steven. *Learning from Las Vegas*, first edition. Cambridge, MA: MIT Press, 1972.

——. *Learning from Las Vegas: The Forgotten Symbolism of Architectural Form*, revised edition. Cambridge, MA: MIT Press, 1977.

Wang, Ming-Hung. "Factory-villa: a case of the emergence of type," *IAPS 12 International Conference on Socio-Environmental Metamorphoses*, proceedings IV, July 1992.

Wertsch, James V. *Voices of the Mind: A Sociocultural Approach to Mediated Action*. Cambridge, MA: Harvard University Press, 1991.

Wittkower, Rudolph. *Architectural Principles in the Age of Humanism*. New York: Columbia University Studies, 1962.

Wundram, Manfred, Pape, Thomas and Paolo, Martin. *Andrea Palladio, 1508–1580*. Köln: Benedikt Taschen, 1989.

Index

Page numbers in **bold** denote illustrations
Page numbers in *italics* denote notes